W9-AFM-513

Pretty Witty Cakes

BOOK OF

SUGARCRAFT
CHARACTERS

BARRON'S

Contents

It is a pleasure to welcome you to my first cake-decorating book. I am thrilled to be sharing many of my top tips and techniques for creating sugar characters with you.

When I began cake-decorating, I could not find a book that provided full step-by-step tutorials for fondant (sugar paste) characters. As a result, I developed my own methods, which I now use when teaching my students. In the past three years, I have taught thousands of students from 45 countries, both in my classes and online. It gives me so much joy to see a complete novice make a character from start to finish in a short space of time, and I am always delighted to see photos of my online students' work. Those photos and the feedback I receive show me that my methods of teaching really work.

This book has been carefully designed, so that, even if you are a complete beginner, you will be able to make the characters. I have insisted on step-by-step photographs that show you everything—just as I do in my videos and classes. I show you many of my tricks of the trade, which you can apply to any character, and I hope this will give you the confidence to create your own characters from scratch.

Those of you familiar with the Pretty Witty Cakes business will know that it was born in 2010, when I made a dramatic career change following the birth of my first child. They say that children change your life, but I could never have imagined that one day I would have my own cake-decorating book. My two boys —Barnaby, aged five, and Bertie, aged three—are key to everything I now do with Pretty Witty Cakes. My business, the bright colors I use, and the impish expressions, faces, and mannerisms I give my characters all come from observing my children every day. My aim with any character is to make it fun, interesting, and a little bit "witty," in order to inspire the playful side in adults and children alike.

Even if you are a beginner, creating characters doesn't need to take a great deal of time—especially if you are juggling cake-making with running a family or another job. My methods and techniques are simple, so you can achieve them quickly and easily. Everything I make starts as a ball, and all designs are based on simple shapes: ovals, sausages, and so on. If you can roll a ball, you can make any of my characters!

Throughout the book, I have included ideas for setting the characters on a cake. The book is intended as a detailed guide to modeling sugarcraft characters and complementary elements of decoration, and I have used every available space to demonstrate these techniques. I therefore do not include cake recipes, although I have given the size and shape of the cake used next to each completed project.

I have tried to create a book that you will find to be fun as well as an invaluable companion when creating sugarcraft characters. I always encourage beginners to copy my characters to the letter; then, when they are more confident, I urge them to use the ideas and methods they have learned to make their own. Whichever characters you attempt, take your time, follow the step-by-steps carefully, and most of all, have lots of fun making *and* eating them!

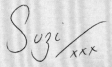

Tips and techniques

Pastes

Fondant (sugar paste)
All the characters in this book are made using fondant. This is also commonly known as sugar paste, but "fondant" is used throughout this book. It is a very versatile paste, making it easy to create many types of characters. Fondant is readily available in cake-supply stores, or you can make your own—there are many fondant recipes on the Internet.

Pre-colored fondant
I generally work with white fondant, which I color myself using gel paste food colors. You can see the various shades that can be achieved using gel paste colors on pages 10–11. However, for very dark colors, or those that require a lot of coloring, I tend to use pre-colored pastes. This includes black, brown, red, and blue.

Gum paste
For detailing on characters—such as items that need to dry hard—I use gum paste, commonly known in the UK as florist paste. Gum paste dries more quickly and much harder than fondant. It is perfect for ruffled skirts, like that worn by the ballerina fairy (see pages 66–71).

Storing paste
When working with any fondant or gum paste, ensure that you keep it well wrapped to prevent it from drying out. Break off the amount you need, then wrap the remainder in a food-safe bag. This will stop air from drying out the paste. If you are storing the fondant for a few weeks, place it in a plastic bag, then in a plastic airtight container. This will help to keep it soft.

Storing completed characters

Unlike paste that hasn't been modeled, never store a completed character in a plastic bag or container. The plastic will cause your paste to sweat and become very soft. The character will then droop, lose its shape, and become very sticky to touch. Fondant characters should always be stored in a cardboard cake box. If stored correctly in this way, they can be made up to four weeks in advance. Remember, the fondant will harden as it dries, so pick up the characters carefully to make sure you don't snap off an arm or a leg!

Preparing your paste

You may find that it is very difficult to model from pure fondant. This will depend on the climate and humidity you are working in. If you wish, you can convert your fondant into modeling paste by adding gum tragacanth, CMC, or tylose powder. Each of these products will make the fondant easier to work with and help it to dry more quickly. The amount you need will vary according to the warmth and humidity in the room, but it is usually about 1 teaspoon per 9 ounces (250 g) of fondant. Knead the powder into the fondant and allow it to settle for 2 hours. You can then work with the fondant in the same way you would have without the powder. Gum tragacanth, CMC, and tylose powder all perform the same role, but most people have a preference. I tend to prefer gum tragacanth. See descriptions of all three substances on the right and overleaf.

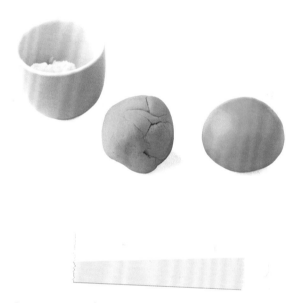

Gum tragacanth

Gum tragacanth is derived from the sap of a plant that grows in the Middle East. The sap is drained from the root of the plant and then dried. This forms a powder that has no taste, smells horrible, but is ideal for thickening fondant. The powder is a light-cream color and is very fine. Avoid breathing in too much because it can induce coughing as it enters the lungs.

CMC

CMC stands for carboxymethyl cellulose. In short, it is the chemical version of gum tragacanth and looks exactly the same. CMC tends to work a bit faster than gum tragacanth and is also slightly cheaper.

Tylose powder

This is another name for CMC, and it is effectively the same thing. It works in exactly the same way.

Coloring paste

To color fondant or gum paste, always use gel paste food colors. Liquid food coloring will change the consistency of the paste, so it should always be avoided. Get a small amount of gel paste food coloring on the end of a toothpick and add it to the fondant or gum paste. Work it between your fingers until it is fully mixed. To make the color darker, simply add more gel paste food coloring.

White vegetable shortening

If you find that your fondant dries out, add a little white vegetable shortening such as Crisco to resoften it. Apply the shortening with your fingertip and work it through the fondant.

Measuring by eye

When making characters, try not to rely too much on weights and measurements set in books. Instead, use your eye to judge the size of a ball, the amount of fondant needed, or the depth of color. Over time, you will create your own style based on your preferences for proportions and design.

Dusting fondant and gum paste

If, after making a character, you find that the color is too bright or looks flat, you can use edible dusting powder (also called luster dust) to bring it to life. Always dust with dry powder and a dry brush. This technique is particularly useful for dusting blusher onto fairies' cheeks or for creating a multitone effect on fish scales or a turtle shell, for example.

Securing parts together

In most cases, you can stick parts together using edible glue or water on the tip of a brush. However, for heavier pieces, or more delicate items such as fairy wings, it may be better to use royal icing. For internal support (for instance, when attaching a head to a body), I use dried spaghetti strands. These can be pushed inside the character to form a spine. Avoid putting inedible items such as toothpicks inside your characters.

Painting on fondant

Painting on fondant is a great way to create a beautiful texture or pattern. There are several ways to make edible paint. My preferred method is to mix a tiny amount of gel paste food coloring (on the end of a toothpick) with about 1 teaspoon of cooled boiled water. The more water you add, the more transparent the color will be. To deepen the color, add a little more gel paste food color. Another method I use is to mix about half a teaspoon of edible dusting powder (luster dust) with half a teaspoon of dipping solution, lemon extract, or vodka. The more tint you add, the thicker the color will be. Vodka dries more slowly than dipping solution or lemon extract due to its higher water content.

Fondant colors

Many of the paste color pots on the market today look black from the outside, so it's hard to tell what the color will look like when added to fondant or gum paste. Here, I've set out 168 samples to demonstrate how the colors will appear in practice.

#		#		#	
1	RS white	57	PME sunny yellow	113	RS Atlantic blue
2	SF super white	58	SF daffodil pastel	114	AM electric blue
3	AM bright white	59	AM electric yellow	115	AM sky blue
4	RS shell pink	60	SF primrose	116	SF navy
5	SF liquorice	61	SF daffodil pastel	117	SF baby blue
6	PME midnight black	62	PME sunny yellow	118	AM navy
7	SF shadow gray	63	RS white chocolate	119	AM royal blue
8	SF shadow gray	64	SF cream	120	RS navy
9	SF black extra	65	PME lime crush	121	SF deep purple
10	AM super black	66	SF lemon/lime	122	AM regal purple
11	SF liquorice	67	SF lemon/lime	123	SF grape violet
12	SF eucalyptus	68	AM electric green	124	PME regal purple
13	RS gray	69	PME lime crush	125	RS amethyst
14	RS bottle green	70	SF mint green	126	AM electric purple
15	PME midnight black	71	SF spring green pastel	127	AM fuchsia
16	AM super black	72	AM mint green	128	AM electric purple
17	SF black extra	73	SF spring green pastel	129	SF lavender pastel
18	RS black	74	SF party green	130	SF grape violet
19	RS chocolate brown	75	SF Christmas green	131	SF deep purple
20	AM chocolate brown	76	RS pastel green	132	PME regal purple
21	SF dark brown	77	SF spruce green	133	AM regal purple
22	SF dark brown	78	SF peppermint pastel	134	RS lilac
23	SF ivory/caramel	79	SF holly green	135	SF lavender pastel
24	RS teddy bear brown	80	AM avocado	136	SF dusky pink
25	AM chocolate brown	81	SF eucalyptus	137	AM fuchsia
26	SF brown pastel	82	SF gooseberry	138	SF pink
27	AM ivory	83	RS lime green	139	SF baby pink pastel
28	SF autumn leaf	84	SF gooseberry	140	PME hot pink
29	AM gold	85	AM avocado	141	RS baby pink
30	SF egyptian orange	86	SF holly green	142	SF claret
31	SF ivory	87	SF spruce green	143	SF burgundy
32	SF autumn leaf	88	SF Christmas green	144	PME berry red
33	AM ivory	89	RS Lincoln green	145	SF poppy red
34	AM gold	90	AM electric green	146	SF ruby
35	SF brown pastel	91	SF mint green	147	SF red extra
36	RS flesh	92	AM mint green	148	AM soft pink
37	PME tiger lily	93	SF party green	149	SF baby pink pastel
38	SF flesh/paprika	94	SF peppermint pastel	150	AM super red
39	SF orange pastel	95	AM teal	151	AM electric pink
40	SF tangerine/apricot	96	RS jade green	152	SF scarlet pastel
41	SF orange pastel	97	SF turquoise	153	PME hot pink
42	PME tiger lily	98	SF sky blue pastel	154	AM electric pink
43	SF flesh/paprika	99	RS duck egg blue	155	AM soft pink
44	SF tangerine/apricot	100	SF navy	156	SF scarlet pastel
45	AM electric orange	101	SF baby blue pastel	157	SF pink
46	RS orange	102	AM navy	158	RS fuchsia
47	SF egg yellow	103	AM royal blue	159	PME berry red
48	AM electric orange	104	RS baby blue	160	SF ruby
49	SF egg yellow	105	AM teal	161	SF red extra
50	SF egyptian orange	106	SF ice blue	162	RS poppy red
51	SF cream	107	AM sky blue	163	AM super red
52	RS yellow	108	AM electric blue	164	SF poppy red
53	SF melon	109	SF sky blue pastel	165	SF claret
54	SF primrose	110	SF turquoise	166	SF ruby red
55	SF melon	111	RS turquoise	167	SF burgundy
56	AM electric yellow	112	SF ice blue	168	SF dusky pink

KEY
SF Sugarflair
AM Americolor
RS Renshaw Sugarpaste
PME PME

Please note: Some colors are listed twice, to show the effect when you use both a tiny amount of paste and a greater amount.

Basic modeling kit

Your number-one tool when modeling fondant characters is your hand. Almost everything in this book can be made using your fingertips, along with a few key tools. Not all of the items listed below are used in every project, but for regular sugarcrafters this is all useful equipment. It is a good idea to look through the step-by-steps to see which of these items are required for a particular project before you get started.

1   Piping gel with Sugarflair ice blue gel paste food coloring
2   Nonstick board
3   Edible glue
4   Scalpel
5   Size 1 sable artist's paintbrush
6   Size 2 sable artist's paintbrush
7   Size 3 sable artist's paintbrush
8   Dried spaghetti
9   Toothbrush
10 Petal veiner / friller tool
11 Foam flower tray
12 Foam flower pad
13 Sugarcraft extruder gun
14 Hair disc for craft extruder gun
15 Rope disc for craft extruder gun
16 Wire cutters
17 Various piping tip shapes for patterning, including size 2, 10, and 103
18 Gum tragacanth (or CMC or tylose powder)
19 White vegetable shortening (Crisco)
20 Oval cutters in various sizes

21 Edible dusting powders
22 Edible gel paste food colors
23 Wedge color shaper
24 Cup chisel color shaper
25 Flat-ended color shaper
26 Pointed color shaper
27 Angle chisel color shaper
28 Round cutters in various sizes
29 Black edible color marker
30 Metal ruler (with measurements to the edge)
31 Nonstick rolling pin
32 Crafted palette knife
33 Smile tool
34 Wheel tool
35 Ball modeling tool
36 Needle tool
37 Stitching / quilting tool
38 Toothpicks
39 Teardrop / rose petal cutters in various sizes
40 Dipping solution, lemon extract, or vodka
41 Small, pointed scissors

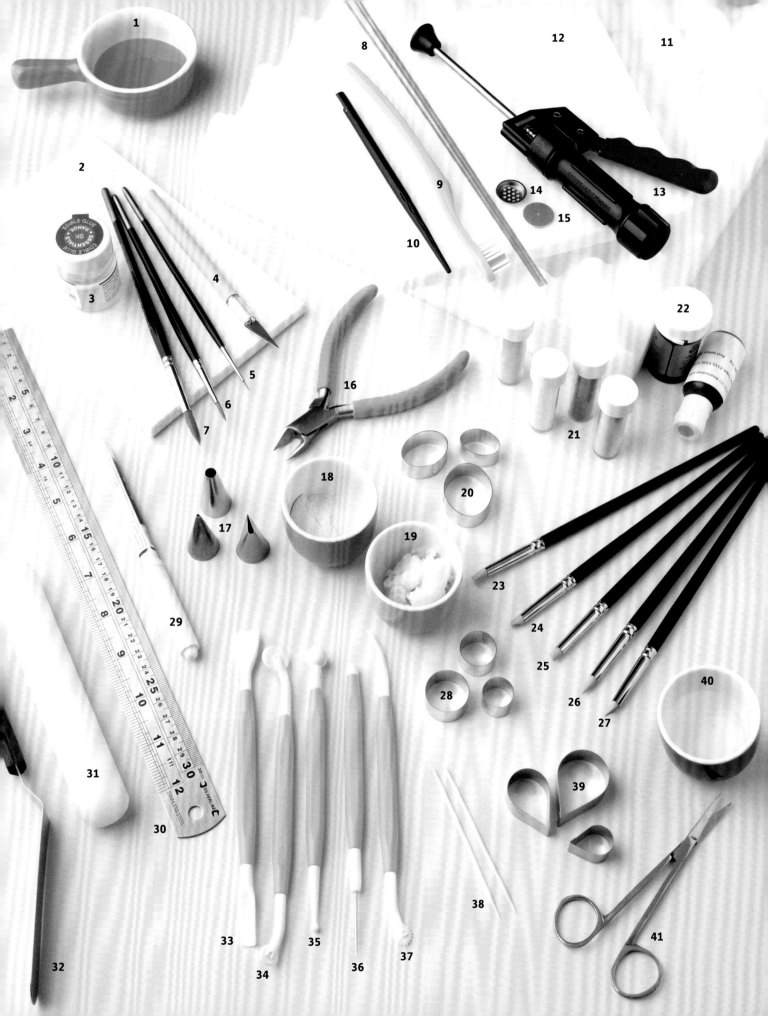

Safari Animals

Flumpy

THE ELEPHANT

YOU WILL NEED:
- Basic modeling kit
  (*see pages 12–13*)
- Fondant (gray, white, black,
  pink, and beige)
- Pink, gray, brown, orange,
  caramel, and black edible
  dusting powder

You can make this character any size you choose. For the size
shown here, use the templates on page 180. The fondant
colors for Flumpy are gray, white, black, and pink. For the
accessories, you will need beige fondant.

1

Roll 6 balls of gray fondant: a body, a head, 2 arms, and 2 legs.

2

Take the largest ball and roll it into a cone shape.

3

Stand the cone with the small end pointing upward. Using your thumb, push down on the front to make a curve and a fat belly.

4

Compare the head ball with the body. The head ball should be about half the height of the body.

5

Place your index finger halfway across the head ball and gently rock it back and forth to make the trunk.

6

Use the tip of your finger to soften the trunk. Make sure it isn't too long (about the same length as the top third of your finger).

7

Push a piece of spaghetti into the body, pushing it all the way to the bottom. Leave a small amount showing at the top. Place the head onto the body. Don't add glue at this stage.

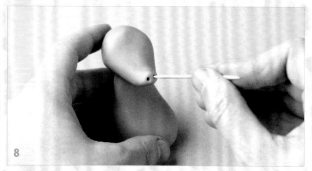

8

Using a toothpick, poke 2 holes in the end of the trunk to make the nostrils.

9

Make 2 holes where you want the eyes to be and make a small hole in the body for a belly button. Add glue with a small brush. Roll 2 equal-sized white fondant balls.

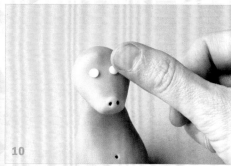

10

Push the balls against the glued holes. The fondant will sink into the holes a little.

11

Add tiny balls of black fondant to make the pupils, then attach to the eyes with edible glue.

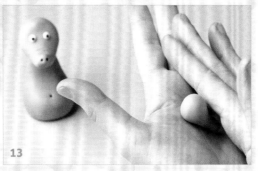

Use the blunt side of a scalpel to make creases in the trunk.

Take the balls of fondant that you put aside for the legs and roll them into cone shapes.

Hold each cone between your thumb and index finger and tap on the table to create a flat foot.

Glue the legs to the sides of the elephant. The backs of the legs (the hip area) should be pushed flat against the elephant.

Use a small ball modeling tool to make 3 indentations in each foot.

Repeat steps 13–16 to make the arms. They should be slightly thinner than the legs, but a little longer so they can rest on the feet. Glue them to the body.

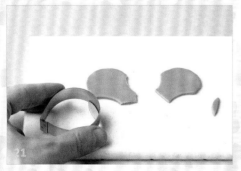

Make indents in the base of the arms as in step 16. Roll 12 equal-sized pink balls, add a dab of glue to the 12 indents, and push in the pink balls until flat.

Before moving forward, glue on the head. Next, roll out a piece of gray fondant on a nonstick board.

Cut out 2 pieces with a teardrop cutter. (Bigger ears make cuter elephants.)

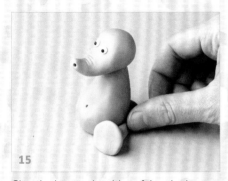

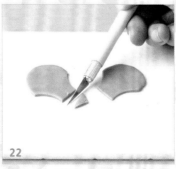

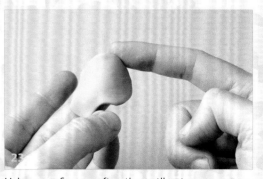

Cut a piece from each side of both tear shapes as shown.

Cut off the points.

Using your finger, soften the outline to remove any jagged edges so the ears are nicely rounded.

24

Roll out some light-pink fondant on a nonstick board. Cut out 2 shapes using the same cutter as in step 20.

25

Slice the edges off the pink pieces, making them smaller than the gray pieces and oval in shape.

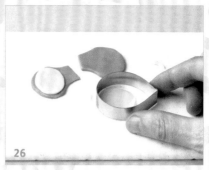

26

Glue the pink pieces into the oval part of each ear, leaving the square edge clear.

27

Apply glue to the square edge.

28

Glue the ears to the sides of the elephant's head.

29

Make creases inside the ears using the back of a scalpel.

TOP TIP

When making an elephant, always position the ears around the side of the head. If you push them up to the top of the head, your elephant will turn into a mouse! Elephant ears can be as big as you wish and will give character to your design.

30

Using the same gray fondant, roll a sausage shape for the tail, making one end more bulbous than the other.

31

Using a scalpel, cut lots of slits in the bulbous end. Glue the tail to the back of the elephant.

32

Roll out a small piece of pink fondant and cut a long strip. Put a dab of glue in the middle.

33

Fold the ends into the middle, leaving loops to form a bow. Cut a smaller strip of fondant and place over the join, gluing into position.

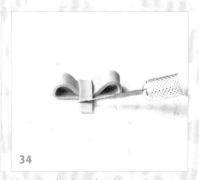

34

Use a scalpel to trim the ends so they are flush with the edges of the bow. Tuck the ends underneath.

TOP TIP
When using dipping solution, be careful not to touch your cake after you have painted it because the dipping solution will not set the paint and you can smudge your pattern. If you are worried about smudging, use lemon extract instead—this sets a little more.

35

Glue the bow onto the elephant's head and dust the creases in the ears with dark-pink edible dusting powder for extra definition. You can also dust the creases on the trunk and around the legs with gray edible dusting powder.

1 Savanna floor

Cover your cake board with light brown or beige fondant. Use a wheel tool to make a random jagged pattern.

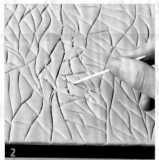

2

Use a toothpick to scrape over the lines and make them rough-edged.

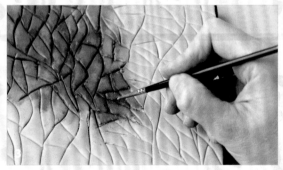

Dust the surface with edible dusting powder in browns, oranges, and caramels. Fill in the cracks with dark-brown dusting powder mixed with drops of dipping solution.

Animal-print pattern

1

Use edible dusting powder in your chosen colors (I used black and pink). Mix with a few drops of dipping solution.

2

Paint pink patches onto the icing on your cake, and outline in black. Ensure the pattern is random and the black edges don't meet.

CAKE DESIGN
For the design shown opposite, I positioned the elephant on a cake approximately 4¼ inches (12 cm) in diameter and 6 inches (15 cm) high. I hand-painted the entire cake and board with the animal-print pattern. If you position your elephant on a cake as shown in this design, make sure you glue her in place with edible glue or a little royal icing.

Jeremy
THE GIRAFFE

YOU WILL NEED:
- Basic modeling kit (*see pages 12–13*)
- Fondant (yellow, white, black, caramel, brown, red, and pink)
- Green gum paste
- Orchid veiner
- 3 long drinking straws
- 18-gauge
- Wooden skewers

You can make this character any size you choose. For the size shown here, use the templates on page 180. The fondant colors for Jeremy are yellow, white, black, caramel, and brown. For the accessories, you will need red, white, black, pink, and brown fondant and green gum paste.

Roll 2 balls of yellow fondant for the body and head.

Roll the larger ball into a cone but elongate the neck, making it as tall as you wish—about 3 inches (8 cm) is best.

Push a spaghetti stick (2 if needed) through the length of the fondant. For a cute giraffe, give him or her a big bottom!

Roll the smaller ball with your finger so that there is a dip in the middle, and the "brain end" is smaller than the "mouth end."

Position the head on top of the long neck, inserting the spaghetti into the fondant (do not stick). Use a small ball modeling tool to create 2 nostrils. To make flared nostrils, pinch the fondant between the ball tool and your finger.

Remove the head to add details to the face. To make a smile, gently push one side of a size 2 tip into the fondant.

Make indentations for the eyes using a small ball modeling tool. With a toothpick, make 2 holes above the eyes for the brown giraffe knobs.

Roll 2 white balls (larger eyes are cuter than smaller ones) and glue them into the indentations made in the previous step.

Roll 2 small balls of black fondant and glue them onto the eyes to make the pupils.

Make some brown fondant (add orange for a caramel tone) and roll 2 small balls.

Roll both balls into cones and pinch to create a little knob at the larger end.

12

Cut off the pointed end of each knob.

13

Put the head back on the body and put a dab of glue into the holes you made in step 7. Attach the knobs.

14

At this point, your giraffe should look like this.

15

Roll small balls of brown fondant and press them flat on a nonstick board. Make the edges irregular.

16

Press the first brown patch onto the body. Use a flat-ended color shaper to smooth down the edges so that they merge with the yellow.

17

Repeat all over the body and head as desired.

18

For the ears, cut 2 yellow teardrop shapes using a cutter ⅝ inch (1.5 cm) long.

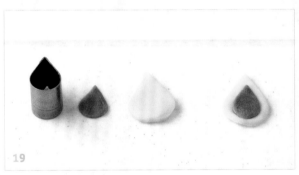

19

Cut 2 smaller brown tear shapes using a cutter about half an inch (1 cm) long; then glue them to the yellow shapes. Ensure that they are closer to the edge at the rounded end.

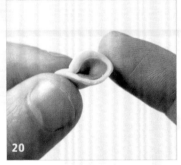

20

Take 1 ear and fold over the pointed end; then curl in the edges.

21

Chop off the pointed end.

22

Repeat steps 20–21 to make the other ear, then attach both ears and point them downward so they look floppy.

23

Using yellow fondant, roll 2 large balls, 2 medium-sized balls, and 1 small ball.

24

To make a leg, roll 1 of the larger balls as shown. This will create a knee area and a sausage shape at each end.

25

Roll out the fondant until the leg is fairly long and thin, making sure the knee isn't too big.

26

Cut off one end to make a flat edge and pinch the other end between your thumb and finger.

TOP TIP
Fondant is very pliable. If you find that it's too stiff or it cracks, reduce the amount of gum tragacanth (or CMC or tylose) used. You can model without the added powders once you're more confident.

27

To make a hoof, roll a small ball of dark-brown fondant.

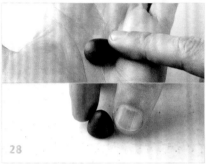

28

Roll into a cone shape, then tap the cone on your work surface to make a flat base.

29

Cut off the top of the cone and discard. Glue the remaining piece to the flat end of the leg to make a foot.

30

Cut a small groove in the front of the foot to create a hoof.

31

Cover the leg in brown patches as you did with the head and body. Use the flat-ended color shaper to smooth down the edges.

32

Make a second leg in the same way, but bend it in the opposite direction.

33

Attach both legs to the base of the body using edible glue.

34

To make the arms, repeat steps 24–32 using the medium-sized balls. The arms should bend more sharply at the elbow.

35

Attach the arms at the shoulder and cross 1 arm over the other.

36

37

38

For the tail, roll the smallest ball into a sausage shape and cut off one end. Bend the tail and flatten the other end with your fingertip.

To make the hair, roll out a small ball of brown fondant into a cone shape and cut off the rounded end.

Cut off the flattened end of the tail. Glue the hair to the other end and make hair lines with a wheel tool. Add patches.

39

40

Attach the tail to the back of the giraffe with edible glue. Let him sit on it slightly. If you wish, you can rotate the giraffe's head as shown. Glue in place once you're happy with the overall position.

Cecil the Snake

1

2

3

Roll out a ball of red fondant into a long, pointed sausage.

Bend the thinner end and raise the fatter end to stand upright.

Use the wide end of a size 2 tip to make a mouth, then make indentations for the eyes using a needle tool.

Roll 2 small white balls for the eyes and glue them in place. Use 2 tiny black balls for the pupils. Roll out a strip of light-pink fondant very thinly and cut out triangles.

Fix the triangles in place along the length of the snake using edible glue.

Your finished snake should look like this.

Coconuts

Roll an oval of white fondant about half an inch (1 cm) wide and ⅝ inch (1.5 cm) long, then place it on top of a rectangle of brown fondant.

Wrap the brown fondant around the oval and close 3 sides. Cut triangles in the open end, then seal. Roll in your hand to smooth out the joins.

To make the "hair" pattern, roll a wheel tool over the surface.

Cut some of the coconuts in half and use a large ball modeling tool to push in the white area.

Use the wheel tool to add texture to the cut side of the brown fondant.

Leaves

Cut freehand large and small leaves from green gum paste.

Create veins using an embosser (here I have used an orchid veiner).

Leave to dry on a curved surface, such as a large nonstick rolling pin, for at least 2 hours and ideally 24 hours.

Tree

Wrap 3 long drinking straws together with floral tape.

Push the straws into the cake all the way to the bottom so that they stand up.

Put 18-gauge floral wire into the straws and bend the tops to make branches. Fill the gaps with wooden skewers.

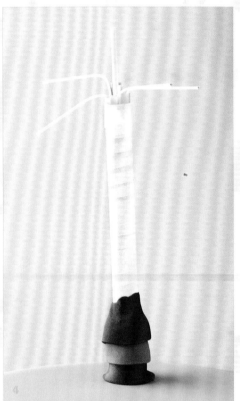

Using brown and light-brown fondant, wrap strips around the trunk. Overlap them and secure with glue as you go up the trunk.

Cover the wires with brown fondant and glue a ball of fondant in the center.

When the leaves are bone-dry, glue 4 large leaves onto the sugar-paste-covered wires.

Build up with more leaves by gluing them to the brown ball of fondant in the center.

TOP TIP

All my characters are based on simple shapes. When I design any character, I build them as a series of circles, squares, and rectangles. Working in this way, anyone can create an animal with human characteristics. Details can be added later.

CAKE DESIGN

The setting I've created here is just one example of how you can position your giraffe. He will work well on any cake design or on a cupcake if made smaller. Here, I've used a cake about 8 inches round and 4 inches high (20 cm x 10 cm). I've covered the cake with green fondant and placed the giraffe under the tree, surrounded by coconuts. You could insert taped straws into a larger plastic dowel before covering in fondant. This ensures that your tree is food-safe by preventing the wire or tape from coming into contact with the cake.

Zachary
THE ZEBRA

You can make this character any size you choose. For the size shown here, use the templates on page 181. The fondant colors for Zachary are white, gray, black, and pink. For the accessories you will need red, yellow, mauve, green, and blue fondant.

YOU WILL NEED:
- Basic modeling kit (*see pages 12–13*)
- Fondant (white, gray, black, pink, red, yellow, mauve, green, and blue)
- Small heart plunger cutter
- Light brown sugar
- Teaspoon

1

Roll 2 white balls—1 large and 1 small—for the body and head.

2

Roll the larger ball into a cone shape. Use your thumb to push down on the front to make a curve. Push a piece of spaghetti all the way to the bottom.

3

Place the smaller ball in your palm and roll one end so that it becomes narrower than the other end.

4

Push the smaller ball onto the spaghetti. Do not glue.

5

Roll some gray fondant to a depth of about ⅛ inch (3 mm). Cut an oval shape about the same size as the wider end of the face.

6

Using your fingertips, squash the oval to make it thinner and larger.

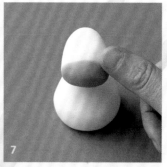

7

Push the oval onto the end of the face and smooth down the edges to merge with the white.

8

Use a small ball modeling tool to make 2 nostrils.

9

Using a size 2 tip, push one side of the large end into the fondant to make a smile (push more for a bigger smile).

10

Use a toothpick or needle tool to make 2 indentations for the ears and 2 more for the eyes.

11

Roll 2 black balls to make the eyes and glue in place. Glue 2 tiny white balls on top, for pupils.

12

Roll 2 equal-sized balls for the ears. Taking each one in turn, pinch one end as shown to form a triangle.

13

Cut off the rounded end of each piece. This will give you 2 soft-edged triangles.

14

Cut 2 small triangles of pink fondant and glue them to the larger white triangles.

15

Glue the ears into the grooves you made in step 10.

16

Roll out a piece of black fondant very thinly, then use a scalpel to cut out long triangles. Don't make them too perfect.

17

Position them all over the body in horizontal bands. They should be a little jagged.

18

Roll a few small balls of black fondant, then shape into long, thin cones.

19

Cut the rounded ends off the cones and glue them between the ears.

20

Your zebra should now look like this.

21

For the legs, roll 2 white balls about ⅝ inch (1.5 cm) in diameter and roll out one end, leaving the other ball-shaped.

22

Tap the ball end on your work surface to flatten the base of the foot.

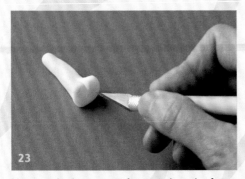

23

Use a scalpel to cut a soft crease into the foot.

24

Place black fondant triangles on the legs like you did with the body.

25

Roll out some black fondant and cut out 2 heart shapes using a small heart cutter. Glue them to the bases of the feet.

26

Glue the legs to the base of the body, tucking them underneath the body slightly.

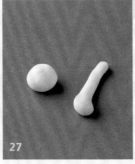

27

Roll 2 white balls about ½ inch (1 cm) in diameter for the arms. Roll out one end.

28

Repeat steps 22–23 to make the arms, then attach heart shapes as in step 25.

29

Attach stripes and a small piece of black fondant to cover the join. Leave to dry for a few minutes.

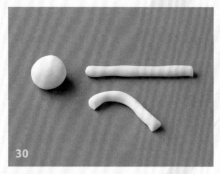

30

While the arms are drying, roll a ball of white fondant and shape it into a tail. Cut off each end.

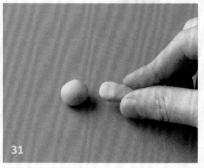

31

Roll a small ball of gray fondant and shape into a cone.

32

Attach stripes to the tail. Glue the flat end of the gray cone to one end of the tail, then mark lines on the gray piece with a wheel tool.

33

Attach the arms and the tail, ensuring that the arms sit in front of the tail. Glue on the head. (Always glue pieces in place as late as possible, only when you're happy with the zebra's position.)

1
Bucket

Roll a cone of red fondant, then cut off the top and bottom.

2

Using a large ball modeling tool, push the fondant against your finger to make a rim.

3

Wrap a thin strip of fondant around the rim of the bucket.

4

Cut a thin strip of yellow fondant and curve it into an arch. Leave it to dry for 1 hour.

5

Fill the bucket with light brown sugar (this resembles sand) and glue the handle in place.

1
Spade

Roll 2 sausages of yellow fondant—1 long and 1 short—and glue them together to form a "T" shape. Roll an oval about ¼-inch (5 mm) thick, then cut off one end.

2

Glue together, then use a large ball modeling tool to shape the inside of the spade.

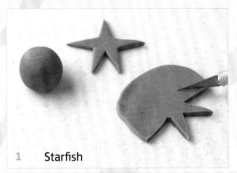

1   Starfish

On a nonstick board, roll out some mauve fondant to ¼ inch (5mm) thick. Using a scalpel, cut out a freehand 5-pointed star.

Gently pinch each point between your thumb and finger to soften the edges.

Texture the surface using a small ball modeling tool.

Make a smile with a tip. Glue on 2 white balls for eyes, with black pupils on top.

Crocodile in the water

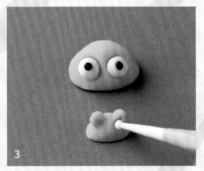

Roll a green ball and cut off one side. Give both pieces flat bases and curved sides. Use a ball modeling tool to make eye indentations on the large piece.

Fill the indentations with 2 white balls, then add 2 tiny black balls for pupils. The pupils should look up toward the zebra.

Add 2 small balls of green fondant to the top of the nose. Make indents with a small ball modeling tool as shown.

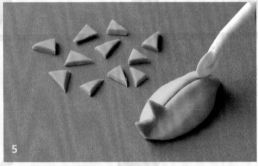

Sea and island

Make a back shape (and a tail, if desired) and pinch along the top to form a visible spine. Make sure this piece has a flat base.

Roll a wheel tool along the spine. Insert small triangles of darker-green fondant into the ridges. You can repeat this along the tail.

Cover your cake or board with light-blue fondant, then paint edible glue over the area where the island will go.

Pour light brown sugar over the glue, building up an island. Pat down the sugar to compress it. Remove any stray granules with a soft, dry brush.

Put some piping gel in a bowl, then add a little ice-blue gel paste food coloring and mix with a teaspoon.

Use the spoon to pour the blue piping gel onto the iced cake or board around the island, until all the blue fondant is covered.

TOP TIP
Piping gel is perfect for creating a water effect. If it is too thick to pour from a spoon, heat it in the microwave in 5-second bursts until it reaches the desired consistency.

CAKE DESIGN
You can set your zebra in the middle of a cake of any size. The piping gel can either sit flush with the top of the cake, or you can leave a slight border.

Maloo

THE MONKEY

You can make this character any size you choose. For the size shown here, use the templates on page 181. The fondant colors for Maloo are brown, beige, white, black, and pink. For the accessories, you will need yellow, white, beige, gray, and brown fondant.

YOU WILL NEED:
- Basic modeling kit (*see pages 12–13*)
- Fondant (brown, beige, white, black, pink, yellow, and gray)
- Small heart cutter
- Green, brown, black, and white edible dusting powder
- Black edible color marker
- Fabric imprint mat
- Bark imprint mat

1

Roll 1 ball of brown fondant for the body and 1 for the top part of the head. Roll a beige ball for the lower part of the head.

2

Roll the largest ball into a cone shape. Using your thumb, press down in the middle to make a fat belly. Push a length of spaghetti through the body as shown.

3

Roll out some beige fondant and use a teardrop cutter to cut out a shape that fits onto the body.

TOP TIP
You can use the templates on page 181 to make your monkey exactly the same size as the one shown here, but if you judge the size by eye, you will start to know by instinct what size balls to use. In time, you will find that you start to make the balls the right size at the first attempt, without measuring.

4

Glue the teardrop shape to the belly. Use a needle tool to make a belly button.

5

Take the medium-sized ball and flatten the top with the side of your thumb.

6

Place the small ball on top (you can apply glue, but this isn't essential).

7

Use the pointed color shaper to blend the edges and create a seamless join. This piece will form the face.

8

Using a heart-shaped cutter, cut out one shape; then cut off the pointed end and discard.

9

Glue the remaining piece to the face as shown.

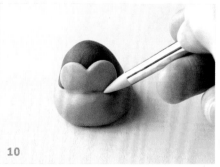

10

Use the pointed color shaper to blend in the straight edge.

11

Make a smile by pressing the wide end of a size 2 piping tip into the face.

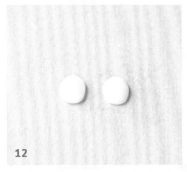

12

For the eyes, roll 2 equal-sized balls of white fondant and press flat.

13

Glue the eyes to the face and use a small ball tool to make indents for the pupils. Roll 2 tiny balls of black fondant and a small ball of pink fondant.

14

Glue the black balls into the indents made in the previous step; then glue the pink ball onto the center of the face to make the nose.

15

Roll out some brown fondant and use a small teardrop cutter to cut out 2 shapes. Roll 2 small beige balls and flatten. Glue them onto the teardrop shapes.

16

Take 1 piece and use your finger and thumb to fold over the pointed end and pinch together. Then gently turn in the rounded end.

17

Cut off the pointed end. This completes 1 ear. Repeat steps 16–17 with the second piece.

18

Using the pointed color shaper, make a hole in each side of the head for the ears to slot into.

Glue the ears into the slots.

20

Monkeys' ears tend to be perky rather than droopy.

21

Place the head on top of the body, pushing it onto the spaghetti support. You can glue the head in place now or wait until later.

22

To make the legs, roll 2 brown balls and shape them into long cones with a ball at one end.

Take 1 leg and bend it in the middle to create a knee, then flatten the end opposite the ball (this will be tucked underneath the body).

24

Gently press the ball-shaped end to create a foot.

25

Using a scalpel, cut 1 big toe and 3 smaller toes (monkeys' feet look more like hands).

26

Use your finger and thumb to round off the edges of the toes. Repeat steps 23–26 to make the other leg, making sure the big toe is on the other side of the foot.

27

Glue the legs in place, tucking the ends underneath the body.

28

For the arms, roll 2 balls of brown fondant into long cone shapes (longer and thinner than the legs).

29

Bend 1 arm in the middle, pinching to make an elbow.

30

Flatten the wider end and gently bend. This will create a hand and forearm.

31

As with the feet, cut 3 fingers and a thumb, but chop off the ends so that the fingers aren't too long.

32

Gently roll the fingers to soften the edges.

33

Gently push the fingers and thumb together. Repeat steps 29–33 to make the second arm.

34

Glue the arms in place at the shoulders. The paste will be soft enough for you to move the arms around until the position feels right.

35

For the tail, roll a ball of brown fondant into a sausage shape. One end should be rounded. Bend the tail.

36

Glue the thinner end of the tail in position at the back (let the monkey sit on it). At this point, check that you've glued all the limbs in place.

Unpeeled bananas

1

Mix some yellow fondant with white fondant to make a pale-yellow ball.

2

Roll into a banana shape, with a soft point at each end.

3

Pinch the top to make a stalk, then use a scalpel to cut off the very end and create a flat edge.

4

Dust both ends with green edible dusting powder.

5

Dust along the banana with brown edible dusting powder.

6

Using a black edible color marker, draw lines along the banana and color in the base.

Peeled bananas

1

Using more of your pale-yellow paste, roll a cone shape and cut off the wider end.

2

Slice the large end into quarters (cutting only halfway through the banana) and gently bend them outwards.

3

Pinch the 4 sections flat using your fingertips.

4

Dust the banana skin with brown edible dusting powder, then use green edible dusting powder to color the base.

5

Add more white to your yellow fondant to make a light yellow. Roll it into a cone shape and glue into the banana skin.

6

Draw lines along the skin and color in the base, using black edible color marker. Your finished bananas should look like this.

Sack

1

Roll a ball of beige or light-brown fondant. Push in the top and pinch around the rim with your finger and thumb.

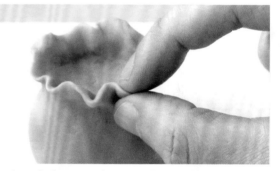

2

To create a gathered edge around the top of the sack, pinch hard all the way around using your thumb and finger (be careful not to break the fondant).

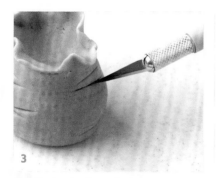

3

Use the back of a scalpel to create creases in the sides of the sack.

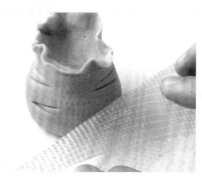

4

Add texture using a fabric imprint mat or a piece of fabric with a raised pattern.

5

Dust the creases with brown edible dusting powder.

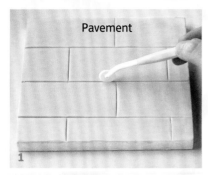

Pavement

Cover a square cake board with gray fondant. Using a wheel tool, draw on the paving bricks (use a ruler if necessary).

Mix black edible ink with dipping solution, lemon extract, or vodka to achieve paint consistency. Paint in between the bricks.

Dust the bricks with black, gray, and white edible dusting powder to create shading. Make them darker near the painted lines, lighter in the middle.

TOP TIP

When making accessories, add about 1 teaspoon of gum tragacanth, CMC, or tylose powder to 9 oz (250 g) of fondant to help it dry faster. This will make it easier to manipulate tiny details.

Wood for the box

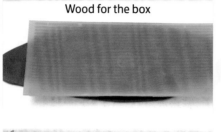

Roll out some brown fondant and cover with a bark imprint mat.

Put pressure on the mat to transfer the pattern to the fondant.

3

Cut the fondant into about 20 strips and attach a small ball of brown fondant to each end. Apply the strips to your cake as shown opposite.

CAKE DESIGN

In the picture opposite, I have used a sharp-edged cake (about 6 inches square and 4 inches high/15 cm x 10 cm) to provide the box shape. I achieved this using 3 layers, which I filled with ganache. I covered the cake in beige fondant and left it to dry for 24 hours until firm. I then placed the wood strips around the sides of the cake, letting the top strip sit ¼ inch (5 mm) higher than the edge of the beige fondant. I left the wood strips to dry before placing the cake on the pavement board. The board required at least 24 hours to dry and firm up. Finally, I added the monkey and bananas.

Ariel

THE LION

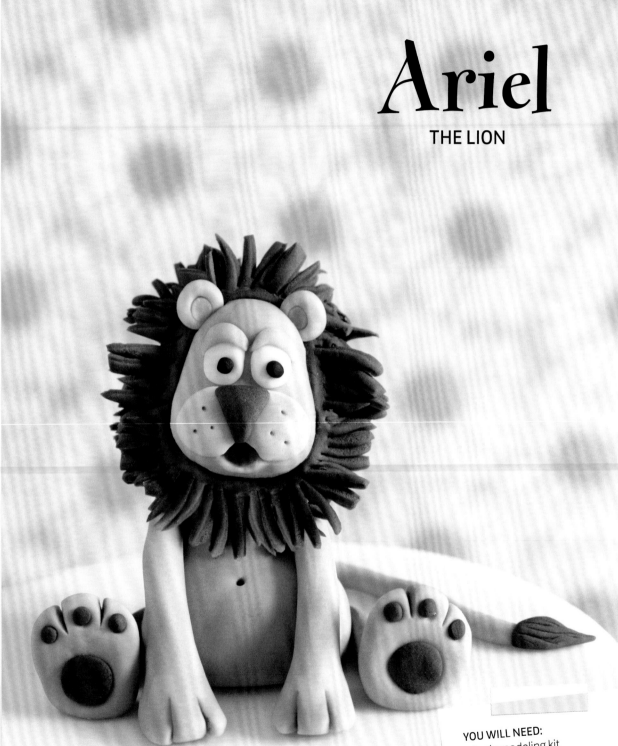

You can make this character any size you choose. For the size shown here, use the templates on page 181. The fondant colors for Ariel are beige, brown, pink, white, and black. For the accessories, you will need gum paste in various shades of green.

YOU WILL NEED:
- Basic modeling kit (*see pages 12–13*)
- Fondant (beige, brown, pink, white, and black)
- Soft pink and light brown edible dusting powder
- Shades of green gum paste
- Leaf or orchid veiner
- Gel paste food coloring in shades of green

Roll 2 balls of beige fondant for the body and head.

Roll the larger ball into a cone shape.

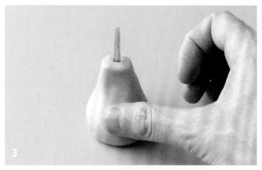

Push a spaghetti stick vertically through the fondant to create a support. Press the middle with your thumb to make a big, round belly.

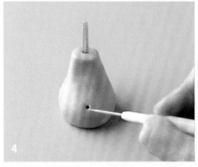

Make a belly button using a needle tool or toothpick.

Roll the smaller ball into a cone shape.

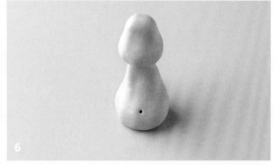

Place the head on top of the body, pushing it onto the spaghetti. Don't glue it in position at this stage. Use your thumb to flatten the area where the eyes will go.

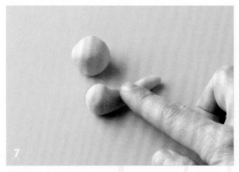

Roll 2 balls of beige fondant for the legs. Roll one half of each ball into a long cone shape, leaving a ball at the other end.

Take the first leg and pinch the ball-shaped end between your thumb and finger to make a flat foot.

Using a scalpel, cut 2 grooves in the foot to shape the paw.

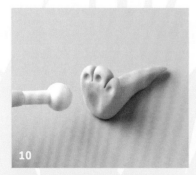

Using a ball modeling tool, make a small indentation in the base of each toe and a large indentation in the sole of the foot.

Roll 1 large brown ball and 3 smaller ones. Glue them into the indentations and press the edges flat using a flat-ended color shaper.

Repeat steps 8–11 to make the second leg. Glue both back legs in place at the base of the body.

13 Roll 2 balls of beige fondant for the arms. Roll out each piece to form a long sausage shape with a ball at one end.

14 Taking one arm, squash the ball slightly and pinch it upward to form a front paw.

15 Using a scalpel, make 2 cuts in the paw. Repeat steps 14–15 to make the other arm.

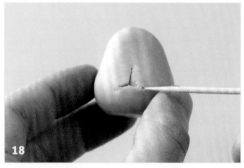

16 Glue the arms in position at the shoulders.

17 Remove the head from the body and use a needle tool to make 2 indentations for the ears.

18 Using a toothpick, mark the outline for the top of the mouth as shown.

19 Use a scalpel to cut out the mouth and remove the fondant from inside the mouth.

20 Using a pointed color shaper and the back of your thumb, soften and smooth out the lips and inside the mouth.

21 Roll 2 balls of beige fondant for the ears and make an indentation in each one with a small ball modeling tool.

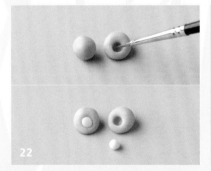

22 Roll 2 small balls of pink fondant. Put glue inside the indentations you made in step 21 and attach the pink balls.

23 Glue the ears into the indentations you made in step 17.

24 Roll out some light-beige fondant. Using a teardrop cutter, cut out 2 shapes and remove the tips—these will form the muzzle around the mouth.

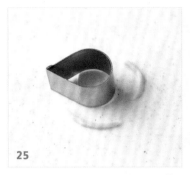

25

If the pieces are too large, slice off some fondant with the cutter.

26

You should be left with 2 shapes that meet in the middle and mirror each other as shown.

27

Glue the shapes above the mouth, covering the top lip. Make holes with a needle tool to represent whiskers. (To make it easier to work on the face, put the head back on the body.)

28

To make the nose, roll a ball of brown fondant and pinch it between your thumb and finger to make a soft-pointed triangle.

29

Glue the nose in position so that the bottom point touches the top of the mouth.

30

Roll oiut 2 equal-sized white balls for the eyes. Glue them into position and press flat. For lions, oval eyes work better than round eyes.

31

Roll out 2 eyebrows and glue them to the tops of the eyes. Use a small ball modeling tool to make indentations in each eye for the pupils.

32

Roll 2 tiny balls of black fondant for the pupils and glue in place. At this point, glue the head in position.

33

For the mane, cut out 3 strips of brown fondant and glue in place as shown. (This method is much easier than trying to attach 1 long piece.)

34

Using a sharp pair of scissors, cut around the mane, thus disguising the lines from the individual pieces of fondant.

35

If you want your lion to have a thicker mane, add a second layer of hair behind the first in the same way.

For the tail, roll a ball of beige fondant into a sausage shape and slice off one end to create a flat edge.

Shape a ball of brown fondant into a cone and attach it to one end of the tail. Use a wheel tool to give the tail tip the texture of hair.

Glue the tail to the base of the lion so that he sits on it.

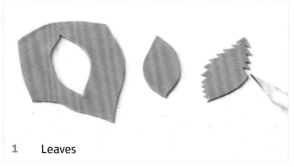

1   Leaves

Roll out some green gum paste on a nonstick board. Using a scalpel, cut out a freehand leaf shape.

Brush some light-pink edible dusting powder onto the lion's cheeks. Use light-brown edible dusting powder to shade under the arms and the darker creases in his body.

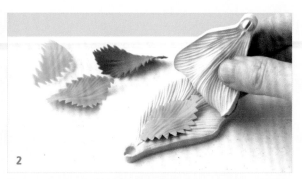

2

Emboss the leaf with a leaf or orchid veiner, then twist. Leave to dry for at least 2 hours and ideally 24 hours. Repeat using other shades of green. Scatter around the lion.

Grass

1

In a tray, mix various shades of green gel paste food coloring with a little water to a watercolor consistency. Paint onto the dry fondant (see Top Tip, right).

TOP TIP
To paint onto fondant icing, mix gel paste food coloring with water and use it as you would watercolors. Avoid the use of shortening when rolling out your fondant because this will prevent the paint from adhering to the icing.

Fairy Friends

Matilda

THE FAIRY

YOU WILL NEED:
- Basic modeling kit (*see pages 12–13*)
- Fondant (white, flesh, purple, black, and brown)
- Petunia cutter and veiner set
- Gum paste (white and purple)
- Large butterfly cutter
- Snowflake luster dust
- Edible dusting powder (soft pink and purple)
- Tiny-details mold
- Lilac metallic edible food paint
- Butterfly plunger cutter
- Sheet of paper
- Royal icing
- Garret frill cutter

You can make this character any size you choose. For the size shown here, use the templates on page 183. The fondant colors for Matilda are white, flesh, purple, black, and brown. For the accessories, you will need brown fondant and white and purple gum paste.

Matilda
THE FAIRY

YOU WILL NEED:
- Basic modeling kit (*see pages 12–13*)
- Fondant (white, flesh, purple, black, and brown)
- Petunia cutter and veiner set
- Gum paste (white and purple)
- Large butterfly cutter
- Snowflake luster dust
- Edible dusting powder (soft pink and purple)
- Tiny-details mold
- Lilac metallic edible food paint
- Butterfly plunger cutter
- Sheet of paper
- Royal icing
- Garret frill cutter

You can make this character any size you choose. For the size shown here, use the templates on page 183. The fondant colors for Matilda are white, flesh, purple, black, and brown. For the accessories, you will need brown fondant and white and purple gum paste.

1. Roll a ball of white fondant for the body.

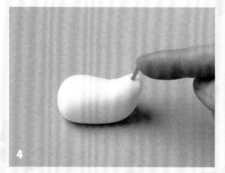

2. Shape the ball into a cone about 1½ inches (4 cm) long. Lay it on its side.

3. Turn up the narrower end of the cone slightly.

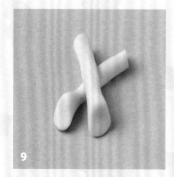

4. Push a length of spaghetti into the turned-up end of the fondant, leaving a short piece showing.

5. For the legs, roll 2 balls of flesh-colored fondant. Shape each one into a long cone.

TOP TIP

When making a fairy, keep the underlying body and head fairly small, since the clothing and hair will dramatically increase the overall size.

6. Take 1 leg and bend the bulbous end into a foot shape, creating a flat heel and pulling the toe area forward.

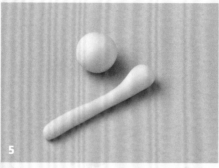

7. Turn the leg over and pinch the heel to make it narrower than the front of the foot.

8. Repeat steps 6–7 to make the other foot. Lay both legs with the feet facing downward and pull the toes back a little.

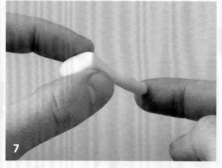

9. Cross the legs and check that you have the toes pointing the right way.

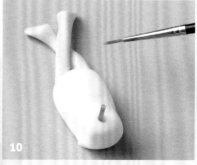

10. Attach the legs to the back of the body using edible glue.

11. For the dress, roll out some purple fondant and cut out some flower shapes using a petunia cutter.

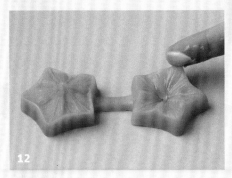

12

Line a petunia veiner with shortening to prevent the fondant from sticking to it.

13

Place a petunia shape in the veiner and press.

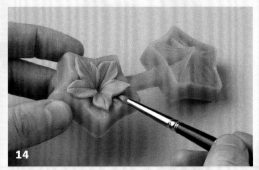

14

Open the veiner and remove the flower using a soft brush.

15

Cut off all the petals, then remove all the pointed ends from the middle area.

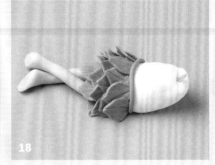

16

Glue the petals around the body, overlapping them a little.

17

Add more petals, working up the body, until you reach the waist. Cover the final row with a thin length of fondant.

TOP TIP

When making fairies, you will often find that you need props to help their arms and legs stay in place. In the case of Matilda, her arms are not actually supporting her body; the body holds itself up. Make sure that small limbs do not carry too much weight.

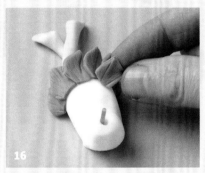

18

From the side, your fairy should look like this.

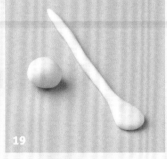

19

For the arms, roll 2 balls of flesh-colored fondant and shape them into cones. Flatten the bulbous ends.

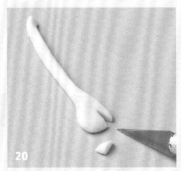

20

Taking 1 arm, cut out a triangle from the flattened area to make a thumb. Smooth out the cut edges.

21

Bend the arm, and put a small ball modeling tool between the fingers and thumb to make space to fit a pencil. Make 2 more petunia petals for the sleeves.

22

There is no need to make a thumb for the second hand. Glue the arms in place and cover the joins with the petal sleeves as shown.

23

Roll out a sausage of white fondant and glue it along the fairy's back as shown.

24

Roll out some white gum paste and cut out a butterfly shape.

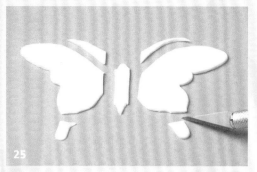

25

Cut off the wings, then remove the top and bottom sections as shown.

26

Cut out holes of different shapes and sizes, using a selection of tips.

27

Dust the wings with snowflake luster dust.

28

Push the wings into the strip of white fondant. You shouldn't need glue, but you can add a little to each wing before attaching if you wish.

29

At this stage, your fairy should look like this.

TOP TIP
Never glue a fairy's head in position until the very end; otherwise, you will keep having to remove it in order to add clothing.

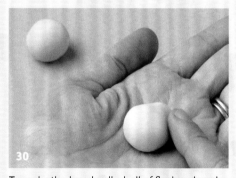

30

To make the head, roll a ball of flesh-colored fondant. Mold it into an egg shape.

31

To make the bridge of the nose, gently press with your right thumb to make a indentation between 10 o'clock and 4 o'clock.

32

With your left thumb, make an indentation between 2 o'clock and 8 o'clock as shown.

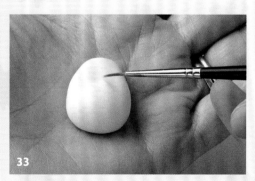

33

Roll a small ball of flesh-colored fondant and glue it to the peak that you've created to make the nose.

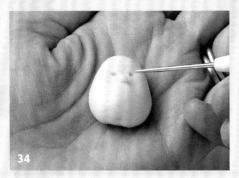

34 Use a needle tool to make 2 holes for the eyes.

35 Place the head on the fairy. With the wide end of a size 2 tip, make a smile, ensuring that it's not too low (hence, add the head first).

36 Remove the head again, then attach 2 white fondant balls to make the eyes. Press them flat as you glue them in place.

37 For the pupils, roll 2 tiny balls of black fondant and glue them onto the eyes. Alternatively, use black nonpareils.

38 Dust the cheeks with pink edible dusting powder, using a small, soft brush.

39 Glue the head in place and add glue to the scalp.

40 Put some brown fondant into a sugarcraft extruder gun with a hair disc attached; then squeeze to produce brown hair.

41 Lay the extruder flat on the work surface, then cut the hair away using scissors.

TOP TIP
When making hair using fondant and a sugarcraft extruder gun, ensure that you arrange the hair in its final position before it dries. Once the thin strands of fondant dry, they become very fragile and will snap if moved.

42 Glue some hair over one side of the head.

43 Glue hair onto the other side.

44 Cut the hair to your desired length.

45

With purple gum paste or fondant, make a tiny bow using a bow mold.

46

Bend the mold back to release the bow.

47

Glue the bow to the hair as shown.

Pencil and paper

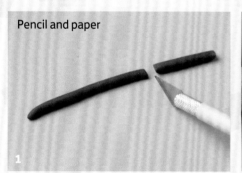

1

To make a pencil, roll out a sausage of brown fondant, and cut to the required length.

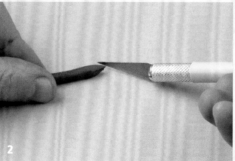

2

Cut 1 end into a point. Keep the cut fairly rough so that it looks handmade.

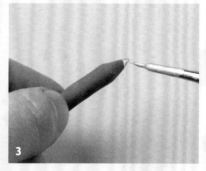

3

Paint the tip of the pencil with lilac metallic food paint.

4

Put a dot of paint at the other end of the pencil for the base of the pencil lead.
Put the pencil in the fairy's hand.

TOP TIP
To make the fairies look petite, it's a good idea to use oversized accessories. Giant pencils, thread spools, and books all work well.

5

Cut out a rectangle of white gum paste. Ruffle the edges and paint wavy lines using lilac metallic food paint.

Butterflies

1

Roll out some purple gum paste, and cut out some butterfly shapes using a plunger cutter.

2

Bend the butterflies in the middle, and place them in folded paper. Leave to dry for at least 2 hours, ideally overnight.

3

When the butterflies are dry, dust with purple edible dusting powder.

4

Use royal icing to attach the butterflies to the side of your cake, then pipe 3 little dots of royal icing along the middle of each one to make the body.

Swags and border

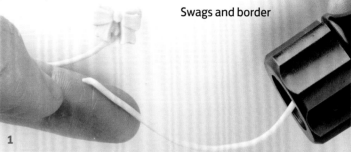

1

Pipe lines of gum paste around the cake using a size 1 piping tip or a sugarcraft extruder gun. If using the latter, glue the paste at each drop. Using a bow mold, make some little bows to cover the joins.

2

For the border, roll out some purple fondant and use a garrett frill cutter to cut out a wide frill long enough to go all the way around the cake.

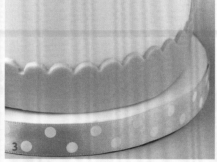

3

Glue the frill around the base of the cake as shown.

CAKE DESIGN

Here, I placed Matilda on a cake measuring about 4½ inches round and 6 inches high (12 cm x 15 cm). This gave enough space for some decoration on the sides of the cake. With fairies, I try to match the flavor of the cake to the color of the fairy. In this case, I added a subtle lavender flavoring to the buttercream.

Eden
THE FAIRY

YOU WILL NEED:
- Basic modeling kit (*see pages 12–13*)
- Fondant (pink, flesh, white, black, brown, and blue)
- Small heart cutter
- Light-pink edible dusting powder
- Gum paste (white, pink, and blue)
- Large butterfly cutter
- Butterfly wing imprint mat
- Snowflake luster dust
- Small blossom cutter

You can make this character any size you choose. For the size shown here, use the templates on page 182. The fondant colors for Eden are pink, flesh, white, black, and brown. For the accessories, you will need white and blue fondant, and white, pink, and blue gum paste.

1

Roll a ball of pink fondant for the body and a flesh-colored ball for the head.

2

Roll the pink ball into a cone and insert a length of spaghetti as shown.

3

Roll the flesh-colored fondant into an egg shape. Uniquely, a fairy's mouth is at the larger end.

TOP TIP
When working with 3-dimensional figures, resist the urge to draw on features; these will be 2-dimensional and won't look as good as molded ones.

4

Use your right thumb to create an indentation between 10 o'clock and 4 o'clock.

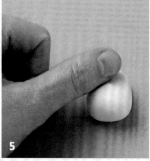

5

Use your left thumb to make an indentation between 2 o'clock and 8 o'clock as shown.

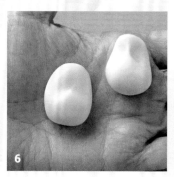

6

You're aiming for the shape on the left. Try not to get the angle wrong or press too hard.

7

Roll a small ball of flesh-colored fondant and glue it to the peak that you created to make the nose.

8

Using the wide end of a size 2 tip, make a smile.

9

Use a needle tool to make 2 holes for the eyes. Make sure everything is in the correct place and in proportion before you proceed.

10

Position the head on the spaghetti (don't glue it), and glue on 2 white balls for the eyes. Press them flat.

11

Glue 2 black fondant balls onto the eyes for the pupils, or use black nonpareils.

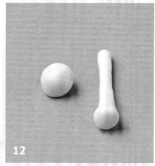

12

For the legs, roll out 2 flesh-colored balls into sausages, keeping a ball at 1 end.

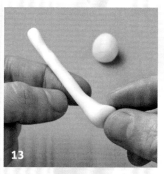

13

Take 1 leg, and pinch up the bulbous end to make a foot shape. Don't make it too flat.

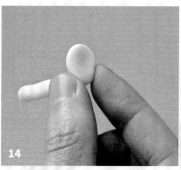

14

Pinch the base of the foot so that the ankle end is thinner than the toe end.

15

Repeat steps 13–14 to make the other leg; then glue both legs to the body.

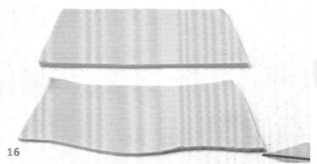

16

To make the dress, roll out some pink fondant (or gum paste, if you find this easier to work with), and cut out a piece with a wavy line along the base.

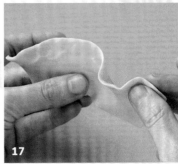

17

Pinch the edge of the fondant, or paste to give it a frilled effect.

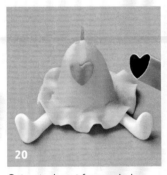

18

Glue the dress around the body, with the join at the back. Roughly smooth out the seam with your finger (this will be covered).

TOP TIP

Where possible, try to make your fairy clothes from fondant, since this will be nice to eat. If the dress is very fiddly, you can use gum paste, or half fondant and half gum paste. This will make the paste firmer and therefore easier to work with.

19

When the dress is in place, gently shape the skirt using a soft brush.

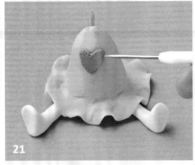

20

Cut out a heart from a darker-pink fondant, and glue this to the front of the dress.

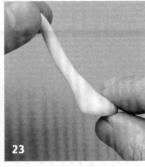

21

Using a needle tool, mark dots around the outside of the heart to resemble stitching.

22

For the arms, roll 2 balls of fondant, just as you did for the legs, but smaller.

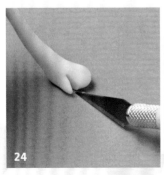

23

Take 1 arm and pinch the bulbous end as shown, to make a hand.

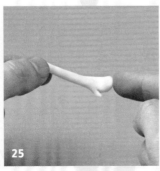

24

Using a scalpel, cut a small triangular piece out of the hand to make a thumb.

25

Soften the edges of the thumb and the hand.

26

Repeat steps 23–25 to complete the other arm; then glue the arms in place.

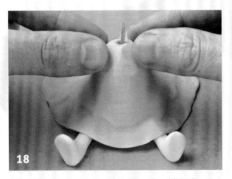

27

To make the sleeves, cut out 2 pieces of fondant as shown.

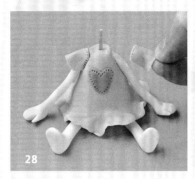

28

Glue the sleeves to the tops of the arms (*see Top Tip, below right*).

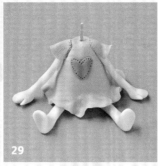

29

Mark dots around the sleeves, using a needle tool.

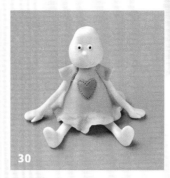

30

At this stage, you can glue on the head.

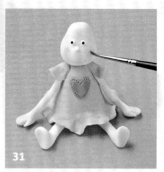

31

Gently dust the cheeks with pink edible dusting powder, using a size 1 or 2 brush.

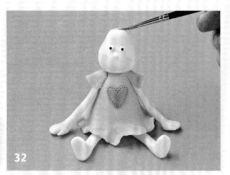

32

Cover the head with edible glue, ready to attach the hair (starting at the back of the head).

33

Make hair using brown fondant and a sugarcraft extruder gun with a hair disc. *How to use a craft extruder gun: page 56.*

TOP TIP
If the sleeves are sitting too flat on the arms, place a small ball of fondant underneath each one before gluing them to the arms.

34

Glue the second bunch of hair on one side of the head.

35

Attach a third bunch of hair on the other side of the head.

36

Use scissors to cut the hair as desired.

37

Using edible glue, attach a small flower to the hair.

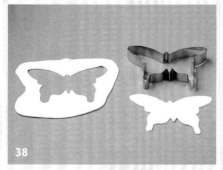

38

To make the wings, roll out some white gum paste and cut out a butterfly shape.

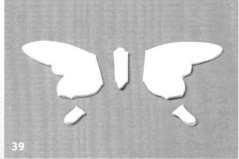

39

Cut off the wings, then remove the bottom tips.

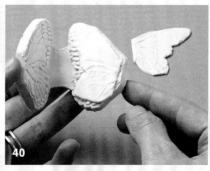

40

Emboss the wings by pressing them in a butterfly wing imprint mat.

41 Cut out holes of different sizes, using a selection of tips.

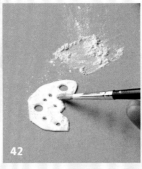

42 Dust the wings with snowflake luster dust.

43 Glue the wings in place in between the central strands of hair. If the wings need extra support, glue a ball of fondant to the fairy's back, then glue the wings to that.

44 Your finished fairy should look like this.

Bunting

1 You'll need a craft extruder gun and a disc with a single hole in it. Fill the gun with pink gum paste.

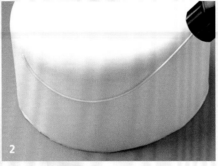

2 Pipe long lines of paste and glue them to the side of the cake at the beginning and end of each length.

3 Cut a series of triangles from gum paste.

4 Glue the triangles along the base of the lengths of paste.

5 Use small flowers to cover the joins between the lengths of paste.

CAKE DESIGN
For the picture opposite, I made a cake of approximately 7 inches round and 4 inches high (18 cm x 10 cm). This gives enough room to decorate the sides with bunting. You could add more small daisies to the cake board if desired.

Darcie
THE FAIRY

You can make this character any size you choose. For the size shown here, use the templates on page 182. The fondant colors for Darcie are white, flesh, blue, black, yellow, and pink. For the accessories, you will need brown, blue, and pink fondant and white gum paste.

YOU WILL NEED:
- Basic modeling kit (*see pages 12–13*)
- Fondant (white, flesh, blue, black, yellow, pink, and brown)
- White gum paste
- Large butterfly cutter
- Snowflake luster dust
- Small blossom cutter
- Light-pink edible dusting powder

1

Roll out a ball of white fondant into a cone shape.

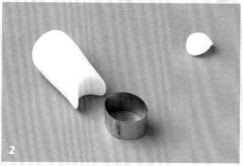

2

Lay the cone on its side and, using an oval cutter that's narrower than the top of your cone, cut out a third of an oval shape.

3

Using your finger and thumb, smooth out the cut area to ensure there are no jagged edges.

4

To create a neck, roll a flesh-colored ball of fondant, and shape it into a cone.

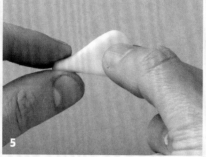

5

Flatten the cone a little so that it's about ¼ inch (5 mm) thick.

TOP TIP
It's a good idea to make the fairy's body the same color as the clothing (rather than flesh color), since the body usually doubles up as the dress.

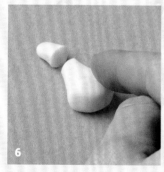

6

Cut off and discard the narrow end, then glue the neck into the curve made in step 2.

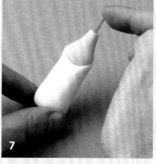

7

Push a length of spaghetti through the body down to the base of the fondant.

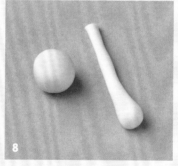

8

To make the legs, roll 2 balls of flesh-colored fondant and shape them into long cones as shown.

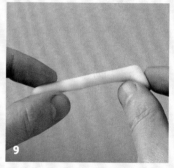

9

Take 1 leg and pinch up the bulbous end to create a foot.

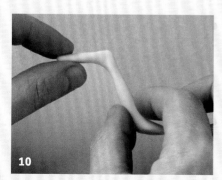

10

Bend the leg about halfway along to create a knee. Repeat steps 9 and 10 to make the other leg.

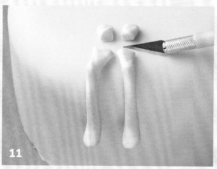

11

Position the legs on the edge of your cake. You may need to remove some fondant from the tops of the legs.

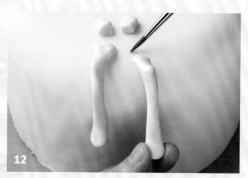

12

Once you're happy with the positioning, gently lift each leg to glue it in place on the cake.

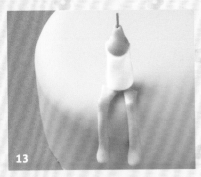

13

Position the body behind the legs and glue in place.

14

Cut a circle of white gum paste about 2 inches (5 cm) in diameter. It should be big enough to make a skirt, but not to cover the knees.

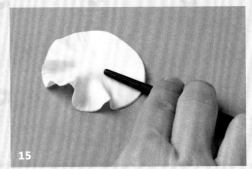

15

Use a petal veiner to ruffle the edges of the paste.

TOP TIP
It's easiest to make very frilly dresses using gum paste, or half gum paste and half fondant.

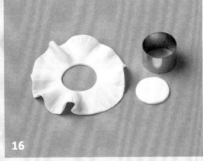

16

Once your paste circle is fully ruffled, cut out a circle from the center. This should be about the same diameter as the body.

17

Slide this layer of the skirt down the body until it sits on the legs. Apply a line of glue above this layer.

18

Repeat steps 14–17 to make 4 more layers (or more if you wish), to build up a tutu.

19

Your fairy should now look like this.

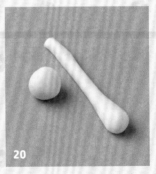

20

For the arms, roll 2 balls of flesh-colored fondant, and shape them into cones.

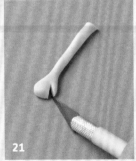

21

Take 1 hand, flatten the palm slightly, and cut out a piece to make a thumb.

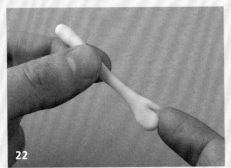

22

Soften the edges of the thumb and the hand.

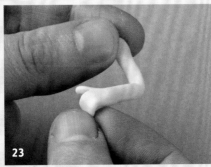

23

Bend the arm; then tuck in the fingers, as if they're gripping. Repeat steps 21–23 for the other arm, making it more relaxed.

24

Glue on the arms at the shoulders—the left hand should be gripping the dress. If the neck seems too long, trim it with a scalpel.

25

Cut a butterfly shape from white gum paste.

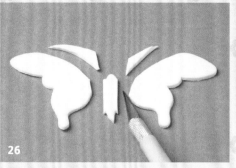

26

Cut off the wings, then remove the top sections as shown.

27

Make different-shaped holes in the wings, using tips or cutters. Dust with snowflake luster dust.

28

Glue the wings onto the body (*see Top Tip, right*).

TOP TIP

If the wings need more support, roll a ball of fondant, and glue this to the back using royal icing. Then use more royal icing to attach the wings to the fondant (it will be covered by hair).

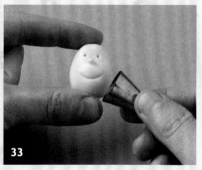

29

To make the head, roll a flesh-colored ball of fondant into an egg shape.

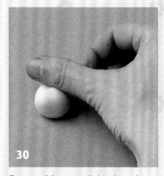

30

Press with your right thumb to make an indentation between 10 o'clock and 4 o'clock.

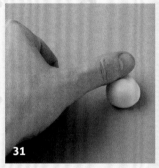

31

With your left thumb, make an indentation between 2 o'clock and 8 o'clock to form a peak.

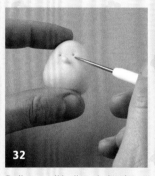

32

Roll a small ball and glue it to the peak to make the nose. Mark out 2 eyes with a needle tool.

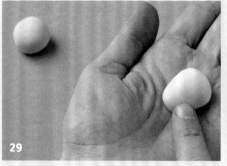

33

Make the mouth with the wider end of a piping tip.

34

Roll 2 white fondant balls for the eyes and glue in place. Add 2 black fondant balls for pupils.

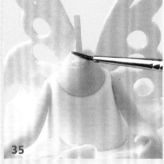

35

Glue the head in place.

36

Apply glue to the top of the head.

37

Make the hair using yellow fondant and a craft extruder gun with a hair disc attached.

Cover the head with yellow hair.

Cut the hair to the desired length, using a small pair of scissors.

Roll out some pale-pink fondant and cut out 6 or 7 small blossoms. Glue little dark-pink balls into the centers.

Glue the flowers around the head.

Use a size 1 or 2 brush to dust the cheeks with soft pink edible dusting powder.

Your finished fairy should look like this.

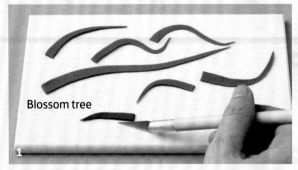

Blossom tree

Cut some strips of brown fondant into various curved and straight shapes to make the branches.

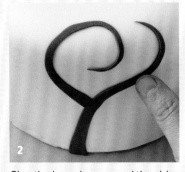
Glue the branches around the sides of your cake.

Decorate with blossom flowers to match the fairy's hair. You can fix these in place using edible glue or royal icing.

CAKE DESIGN
The cake shown here measures about 8 inches round by 4½ inches high (20 cm x 12 cm). You can make the blossom as elaborate or as simple as you like, covering the entire cake and board if you wish, or just the top of the cake. This fairy would also work well sitting on a fondant-topped cupcake with a design like the one shown here.

Bramble & Ben

THE FAIRIES

You can make these characters any size you choose. For the sizes shown here, use the templates on page 183. The fondant colors for these fairies are pink, blue, flesh, white, black, yellow, and orange. For the accessories you will need brown, red, white, and green fondant.

YOU WILL NEED:
- Basic modeling kit (*see pages 12–13*)
- Fondant (pink, blue, brown, flesh, white, black, yellow, orange, red, and green)
- Carnation cutter set
- Butterfly cutter
- Leaf veiner
- Sheet of paper
- Snowflake or pink luster dust
- Light-pink edible dusting powder
- Small blossom cutter
- Calyx cutter set
- Orange or pink edible color marker
- Green royal icing

Roll 2 large balls—1 in pink fondant and 1 in blue—for the bodies.

Roll the balls into cones, about 1½ inches (4 cm) high.

To make the log seat, roll out a sausage of brown fondant, about 1¼ inches round and 6 inches long (3 cm x 15 cm).

Pinch the paste at each end of the log to make a rim.

Roll a wheel tool along the log to create a bark effect. The lines shouldn't be straight.

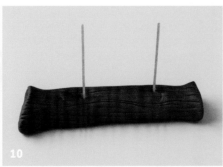

To make the legs, roll 4 balls of flesh-colored fondant into cones as shown.

Take 1 leg and pinch up the bulbous end to create a foot shape.

Pinch the back of the foot so that the ankle is narrower than the toe end.

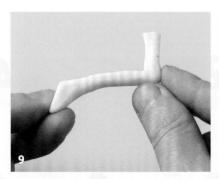

Bend the leg to make a knee.

Before you position the first leg, push 2 lengths of spaghetti into the log where the fairies will sit.

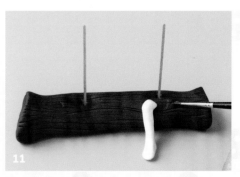

Glue the leg of Ben the boy onto the log, shortening it if necessary.

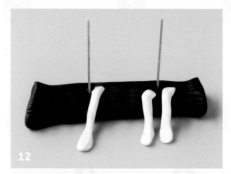

12

Repeat steps 7–11 to make Ben's other leg. Make Bramble's legs in the same way but slightly longer. Glue her first leg at an angle.

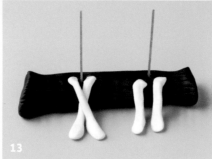

13

Position her second leg crossing over the first leg as shown, then glue in place.

14

Once you're happy with the legs, slide the bodies onto the spaghetti and glue them in place on the log.

15

To make Ben's outfit, roll out a long strip of blue fondant and cut out a row of triangles to make a zigzag.

16

Paint a line of glue around the base of his body and glue on the outfit as shown.

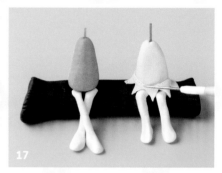

17

Using a needle tool, make dots along the edges of the zigzag to resemble stitching.

TOP TIP
When making fairy wings, experiment with different butterfly cutters and veiners. You can also use leaf cutters to create long, spiral, or pointed wings.

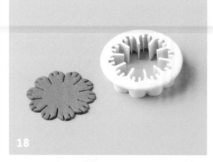

18

To make Bramble's dress, roll out some pink fondant and cut out a carnation shape using a cutter.

19

Ruffle the edges of the carnation with a toothpick.

20

Cut out the center using a number 2 tip.

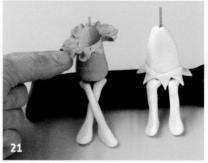

21

Slide the carnation frill over the girl's body, then apply a line of glue on the top.

22

Repeat steps 18–21 to make 3 or 4 more layers. Stick each one to the glue underneath. Adjust the ruffles with a toothpick or soft brush.

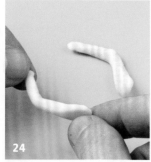

For the outside arms, roll 2 flesh-colored cones, and flatten the bulbous ends.

Take each arm, and bend to make an elbow. Press the palm a little.

Attach the arms as shown, using edible glue. Add a small ball of fondant at the top of Bramble's arm.

Make another carnation shape, as in steps 18–20; then cut out 2 small sections.

TOP TIP
For very small fairies, don't try to cut individual fingers. It will look neater if you just indicate fingers and a thumb.

Glue 1 piece over the ball of fondant at the top of the arm to make a sleeve. Put the other piece to one side.

For the inside arms, roll out 2 cones and flatten the wider ends. Take 1 arm, cut out a piece to make a thumb, and smooth out the edges.

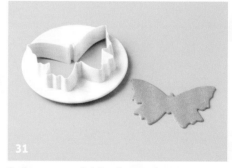

Take the other arm for Bramble, and cut a thumb on the other side of the hand. Attach the sleeve.

Glue the arms in position, bending them so the hands touch. Glue the hands together.

Roll out some pink fondant and cut out a butterfly shape for Bramble's wings.

Emboss the butterfly in a leaf veiner.

Fold a sheet of paper into a accordian shape and place the butterfly on the paper as shown. Leave to dry for at least 2 hours, ideally overnight.

Dust the butterfly with snowflake or pink luster dust.

35

Glue the wings in place on Bramble's back, using edible glue or royal icing.

36

Your fairies should now look like this.

37

For the heads, roll 2 balls of flesh-colored fondant, and mold them into egg shapes.

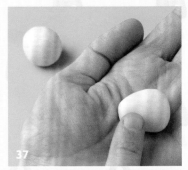

38

Take 1 head, and press with your right thumb to make an indentation between 10 o'clock and 4 o'clock.

39

With your left thumb, make an indentation between 2 o'clock and 8 o'clock, to form a peak.

40

Roll a small ball of fondant. Glue it to the peak to make the nose. Mark 2 eyes with a needle tool.

41

Use the wider end of a tip to make a smile.

42

For eyes, glue on 2 white balls and flatten. Glue the head onto the girl's body; then add pupils.

43

Put yellow fondant in a craft extruder gun with a hair disc. Make long strips. Glue in place.

44

Cut the hair with a small pair of scissors.

45

Using a small brush, dust her cheeks with light-pink edible dusting powder.

46

Use a cutter to cut out a tiny flower and glue it to Bramble's hair.

47

To complete the boy, roll out some blue fondant, and cut out a blue calyx shape using a calyx cutter.

48

Glue this onto the neck, pushing it down over the spaghetti to cover the join between the arms and the body.

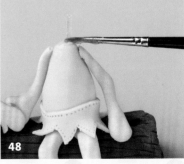

49 Gently press down the calyx ends, and twist it a little if it isn't fully covering the arms.

50 Make another head, following steps 38–42, then glue it to the boy's body.

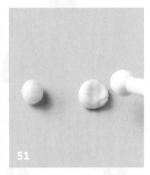

51 Make ears by rolling out 2 tiny balls and indenting the centers with a small ball tool.

52 Glue the ears in place on the sides of Ben's head.

53 Your fairies should now look like this.

54 Put bright-orange fondant into an extruder gun with a hair disc, and put a little glue onto the head. Pipe some hair onto the glue.

55 Let the hair fall so that it's messy, then cut it very short. Add freckles using an orange or pink edible color marker.

56 Your finished fairies should look like this. Leave them to dry for at least 24 hours, then move them to your cake, keeping them in position on the log.

Spike the Hedgehog

To make a hedgehog, roll a ball of brown fondant into a cone and rest it on the work surface to make a flat base.

Make tiny cuts in the fondant, starting a little way along the cone and working up the body.

Add tiny eyes (using the same techniques as for the fairies) and a little ball of red fondant for a nose.

Grass

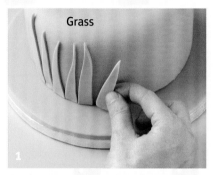

For the grass, cut out pointed strips of fondant in different shades of green, and glue them around the sides of the cake.

Pipe green royal icing around the base to cover the edge of the cake.

TOP TIP
Cover any messy joins with piping or ribbon. Here, I have used a grass disc to cover the join between the cake and the drum. If you make a mistake, use a carefully positioned flower or animal to cover the error.

Toadstools

Roll a ball of red fondant and shape it into a cone.

Cut off the rounded end. The pointed end will make the top of the toadstool.

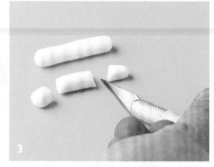

For the stalk, roll out a sausage of white fondant and cut off both ends.

Glue the white stalk to the base of the red cone, and cover in white fondant spots, pressing them flat. Repeat to make more toadstools.

CAKE DESIGN
For the picture opposite, I made a round cake of about 8 inches round and 4 inches high (20 cm x 10 cm). The fairies are sitting in an enchanted forest, so you could use a larger cake to allow room for other animals, including hedgehogs, rabbits, and even elves. You could also decorate the cake board with smaller creatures such as ladybugs and butterflies. I like to use little toadstools, flowers, and hedgehogs as filler elements on cupcakes.

Monsters and Aliens

BLinky

THE ALIEN

You can make this character any size you choose. For the size shown here, use the templates on page 184. The fondant colors for Blinky are purple, white, yellow, red, black, and pink. You will need the same colors for the accessories.

YOU WILL NEED:
- Basic modeling kit (*see pages 12–13*)
- Fondant (purple, white, yellow, red, black, and pink)
- Purple edible dusting powder
- Snowflake luster dust
- Paper towels

1

Roll 5 equal-sized balls of dark-purple fondant, 1 larger ball and 4 smaller balls of light purple, and 1 small white ball.

2

Roll each dark-purple ball to make a sausage ¼ inch (5 mm) in diameter and the lengths shown on the template. Wrap the other balls in a plastic bag.

3

Curve the largest sausage and glue the ends together. Use the pointed color shaper to soften the join.

4

Repeat step 3 for the other sausages. The loops will get progressively smaller. Glue them one on top of the other.

5

Roll the larger light-purple ball into an egg shape to make the head. Glue into the hole at the top of the body.

6

Using a size 2 piping tip, make a groove in the correct position for a smiling mouth.

7

Push a large ball modeling tool into the head to make an eye shape. Press your index finger against the fondant on top of the ball modeling tool to make a lip over the eye socket.

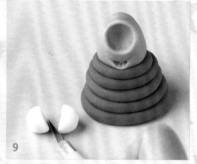

8

Using a toothpick, make an open mouth ready for the tongue to sit in.

9

Cut the small ball of white fondant in half with a scalpel.

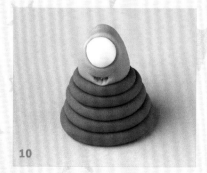

10

Shape 1 of the halves so that it is smooth and round, and push it into the eye socket, gluing it in place.

11

Cut out small circles of yellow and red fondant and roll a small ball of black fondant. These must be small enough to fit on the white eye.

12

Glue on the yellow fondant circle, then the red, and push down with the flat-ended color shaper so they're flush with the white fondant.

13

Glue on the black ball, and push down with the flat-ended color shaper.

14

Add a tiny ball of white fondant to the eye.

15

Take 2 of the small light-purple balls, and press down with the side of your thumb to create a flat half.

16

Apply glue to the flat half of each piece, and slot underneath the body.

17

Make 3 holes in each foot using the pointed color shaper.

18

Use a toothpick to make a slot in each side of the upper body, ready for the arms.

19

Take the remaining 2 light-purple balls and roll them into long cone shapes.

20

Cut a small thumb slit in each cone.

21

Take 1 cone, and use your fingertip to smooth out the thumb and fingers so that they look like a mitten.

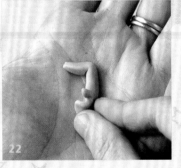

22

Bend the arm to make an elbow, and curve the hand around so that the fingers tuck into the palm.

23

Wrap the thumb over the top of the fingers.

24

Repeat steps 21–23 to make the other arm; then secure both arms in the slots created in step 18 and glue in place.

25

Cut 2 small strips of red fondant; then wrap them around the tops of the arms to cover any messy joins.

26

Using a toothpick, make a row of tiny holes along each red strip to resemble armor.

27

Using red fondant, roll 3 tiny cone shapes. They should be very thin and pointy.

28

Glue the cones to the top of the head. Once fixed in place, bend the ends with your fingertips to make them curl.

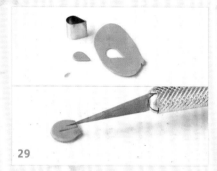

29

Cut out a teardrop shape of light-pink fondant and slice off the point. Make a groove with the back of a scalpel.

30

Put some glue into the hole you made for the mouth in step 8, and push in the tongue.

31

Brush dark-purple edible dusting powder into all the holes in the toes and around the rings of the body.

Doogi

1

Roll a ¾-inch (2-cm) purple ball and shape it into a cone. Cut in half, from the top to the center, as shown.

2

Round off the edges of the cut with your fingers, and insert a length of spaghetti in each side.

3

Roll 2 balls of purple fondant, push them onto the spaghetti, and glue them in place. Make an indentation in each ball with a large ball modeling tool.

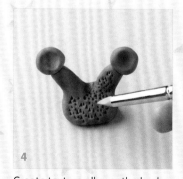

4

Create texture all over the body by gently making marks using an angle chisel color shaper.

5

For legs and arms, make 4 long cones, and flatten the wide ends. Bend as shown, and glue.

6

Make 2 eyes following steps 9–14 for Blinky then you have a little matching friend.

Slugger

1

Slugger is made using the principles you applied to Blinky. Roll 9 purple fondant balls decreasing in size.

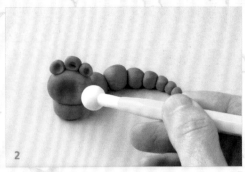

Rocky

2
Glue the balls together, then add a tenth ball to make a head/eye, with 3 small balls on top. Indent the balls with a ball modeling tool as shown.

3
Make 1 eye following steps 9–14 for Blinky; then add 2 legs (*see Doogi, step 5*). Make 4 tiny red cones; glue into the indentations.

1
Using purple fondant, roll out an oval shape, and cut it through the middle from the top to halfway down.

2
Pinch the fondant between your finger and a large ball modeling tool to create 2 eye sockets.

3
For the legs, roll 4 balls of purple fondant into long sausages.

4
Take 1 leg and bend as shown. Pinch at both ends. The larger end is the foot.

5
Repeat step 4 to create 4 legs; then make 2 holes in the front of each foot with a needle tool.

Satin white planet

6
Glue the legs in place as shown.

7
Create eyes following steps 9–14 for Blinky, then roll tiny cones of red fondant to make little spikes. Glue them in place as shown.

1
On your board or cake, add lumps of fondant to create little mountain bumps.

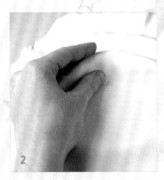

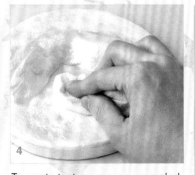

2
Cover the board or cake with white fondant.

3
Mix snowflake luster dust with dipping solution (*see page 9*), and paint onto the fondant.

4
To create texture, press a crumpled sheet of paper towels all over the fondant.

CAKE DESIGN
Blinky and his friends can be used to decorate any cake, cake board, cake tiers, or individual cupcakes. The latter works very well, since each cupcake is related but slightly different. You can create a satin-white planet effect on a large cake, mini cake, or cupcake surface.

Giggles
THE MONSTER

YOU WILL NEED:
- Basic modeling kit
  (*see pages 12–13*)
- Fondant (pink, white, blue, black, yellow, and green)
- White gum paste
- Snowflake and blue luster dust

You can make this character any size you choose. For the size shown here, use the templates on page 185. The fondant colors for Giggles are pink, white, blue, black, yellow, and green. You will also need white gum paste. For the accessories you will need blue fondant.

To make the body, roll a large ball of pink fondant.

Roll the ball into an egg shape.

Using a teardrop cutter about 1¼ inches (3 cm) in length, cut out a lighter-pink fondant shape.

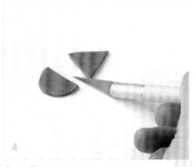

Cut off the pointed end of the teardrop shape.

Using the round end of the cutter, cut a crescent from the flat side to make a smiling mouth.

Glue the mouth to the body.

Using more lighter-pink fondant, roll 2 long, thin sausages. Glue one around the bottom of the mouth and the other around the top.

Trim off the ends with a scalpel.

Make indentations for the eyes and nose using a ball modeling tool.

TOP TIP

By having one feature that stands out more than any other, you will find it easier to create a personality for your character. Choose what attribute is the most representative and make that the main focus.

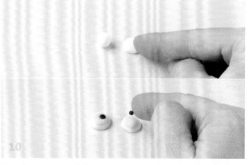

For the eyes, roll 2 white balls and press flat. Roll 2 smaller pale-blue balls, flatten, and glue to the whites. Add 2 tiny black balls for the pupils.

Glue the eyes into the indentations created in step 9.

Using yellow fondant, roll a large ball for the nose and glue it in position.

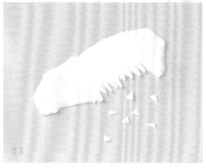

For the teeth, roll out out some white gum paste until very thin, then cut out some tiny triangles.

TOP TIP
For very tiny features such as teeth, use gum paste instead of fondant. It is firmer and will make it easier to pick up and manipulate small pieces without distorting the shapes.

Glue the teeth inside the mouth along the top and bottom lips.

For the hair, roll out about 8 thin, pointy lengths of green fondant.

Glue the hair onto the top of the head.

Your monster should look like this.

To make the ears, roll 2 balls of pink fondant, and form into cone shapes.

Take 1 cone, and push a large ball modeling tool into the wider end to make an indentation.

Roll out a small circle of lighter-pink fondant, and press it into the indentation.

Cut off the point of the cone. Repeat steps 19–21 to make the second ear.

Push a short length of spaghetti into each side of the head to support the ears.

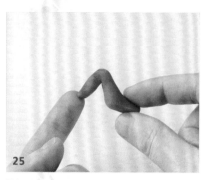

Put some edible glue onto the base of each ear; then push the ears onto the spaghetti supports, making sure they stick to the sides of the head.

For the legs, roll 2 balls of pink fondant, and shape into sausages, leaving a bulbous section at one end about ½-inch (1-cm) long.

Take 1 leg, and bend it to create a knee as shown.

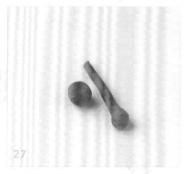

Repeat step 25 to make the other leg, then glue both legs underneath the body so that your monster is sitting on the legs.

To make the arms, roll 2 balls of pink fondant, and shape them into sausages with a ball at 1 end.

Take 1 arm and, using a scalpel, cut out 2 small triangles to create 3 fingers as shown.

Bend the arm to create an elbow; then smooth out the edges of the fingers between your thumb and finger.

Repeat steps 28–29 to make the second arm; then glue both arms in place, below the ears but higher than the mouth.

Your finished monster should look like this.

Diplet

Make a pink droplet shape, and add a face as you did for Giggles (*see steps 3–14*). Make 2 small droplets for the feet and 2 flattened balls for the arms.

Attach a green fondant curl to either side to make the hair.

Peewee and Zilla

To make Peewee and Zilla, or other characters, combine any of the techniques used to make Giggles, and adapt them for each new monster.

Landscape

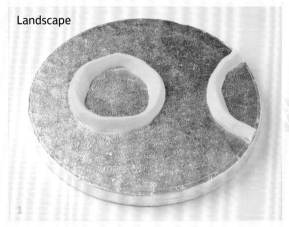

Roll sausages of fondant and place them on a cake board or cake surface to make craters.

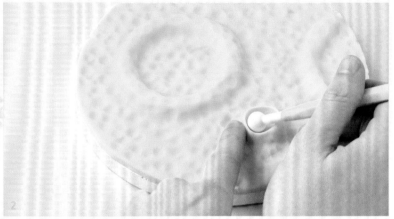

Cover the surface with blue fondant and make a bumpy texture using a small ball tool. To make a small crater, attach a blue ball to the surface and push down inside using a large ball tool, pressing the fondant against your finger to create a thin lip.

Mix snowflake and blue luster dust with a few drops of dipping solution (*see page 9*), and paint over the surface.

To create the water, use piping gel mixed with a few drops of blue gel paste food coloring.

CAKE DESIGN

Putting a monster or alien on a cake is a great opportunity to experiment with texture. Here, I have created a texture for the surface of a swamp or planet. This can be made on a cake, or on a board with the cake itself as the planet. If you intend to create bumps on the surface of the cake, ensure your fondant is quite thick and chill the cake before working so it doesn't change shape when you apply pressure to the surface.

Boppa

THE MONSTER

YOU WILL NEED:
- Basic modeling kit (*see pages 12–13*)
- Fondant (orange, green, purple, yellow, red, black, white, beige)
- White gum paste
- Purple, brown, and gray edible dusting powder

You can make this character any size you choose. For the size shown here, use the templates on page 184. The fondant colors for Boppa are orange, yellow, white, black, green, purple, and red. You will also need white gum paste. For the accessories, you will need purple, green, white, black, and beige fondant.

Roll a large ball of orange fondant for the body.

Using a scalpel, cut out a semicircle to create a mouth.

Cut away the inside of the mouth.

Using your finger and thumb, pinch around the edge of the semicircle to create the lips.

Use a flat-ended color shaper to smooth down any rough areas, and gently press around the inside edge of the mouth.

To make the arms, roll 2 orange balls and flatten into crescent shapes. They should bend in the middle to resemble paddles or flippers.

Attach the arms to the body using edible glue.

Using the tip of a pair of scissors, cut tiny snips into the body and the arms to create a furry texture.

Roll out a thin piece of gum paste, then cut out small triangles with one end cut off to make teeth.

Glue the teeth inside the mouth, about ⅛ inch (3 mm) in.

Roll a ball of green fondant for the nose. Make 2 indentations with a small ball modeling tool for nostrils.

Dust inside the nostrils with purple edible dusting powder.

13

Glue the nose in place above the mouth. Using a needle tool, make 2 holes for the eyes.

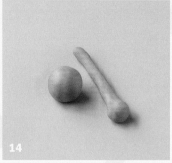

14

To make the legs, roll 2 balls of orange fondant into sausage shapes with a ball at 1 end.

15

Take 1 leg, and bend it in the middle to create a knee.

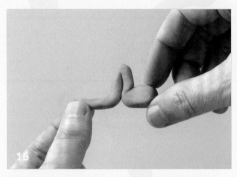

16

The angle of the bend should be increased as shown, making a foot at the ball end and a length of fondant at the other end.

17

Repeat steps 15–16 to make the other leg, then cut off the leftover fondant as shown.

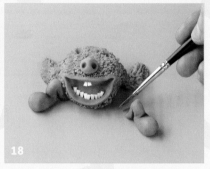

18

Glue both legs in place underneath the monster.

TOP TIP
When making monsters, try to work with complementary colors. These will naturally stand out and give your cake great impact.

19

For the eyes, roll 2 balls of purple fondant. Make a hollow in each ball with a ball modeling tool; then push the edge of the fondant against your finger with the tool to create a lip.

20

Roll 2 balls of yellow fondant and cut off one-third of each ball.

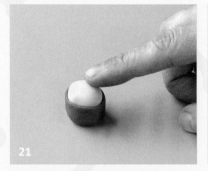

21

Glue the larger yellow pieces into the cavities made in the purple eye sockets.

22

Cut out 2 red circles, glue 2 black balls on top, and add 2 tiny white balls. Glue onto the yellow eyes. Smooth the edges with a flat-ended color shaper.

23

Wrap purple fondant around a piece of spaghetti as shown, then glue the tip into a purple eye socket. Repeat for the other eye.

Push the eyes into the holes made in step 13 (you may need to put a little glue into the holes).

TOP TIP
When working with fondant, keep your fingernails short. It is very easy to dent a finished character with a sharp or long nail. It is also much easier to model with shorter finger nails, since most modeling is done using your fingertips.

Your finished monster should look like this.

Landscape

Place some uneven lumps of fondant around your cake or board (glue in place using cooled boiled water). Brush your board with water.

Cover the cake or board with beige fondant about ¼ inch (5 mm) thick.

Use the small end of a ball modeling tool to create a rock texture all over the fondant surface.

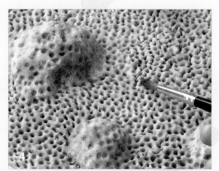

Dust the textured surface with brown edible dusting powder.

Bones

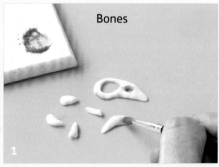

For the bones, use white fondant to make a selection of randomly shaped pieces, then dust with gray edible dusting powder.

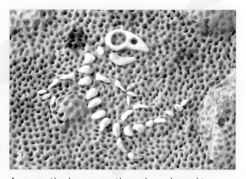

Arrange the bones on the cake or board to create a skeleton shape.

Boggle the purple monster

1 Roll out a ball of purple fondant into a long, pointed sausage, leaving a ball at 1 end.

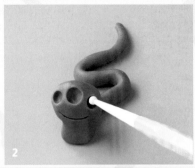

2 Make 3 indentations for the eye sockets with a ball modeling tool. Use the tip of a scalpel or a mouth size 2 nozzle.

3 Add green patches to the monster and smooth down with a flat-ended color shaper.

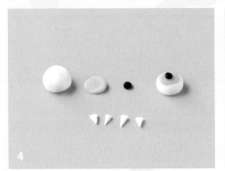

4 To make the eyes, roll 3 white balls, glue on flat green circles; then top with tiny black balls. Make teeth out of gum paste.

5 Glue the eyes and teeth in place using edible glue.

Sludge the green monster

1 Roll out a ball of green fondant into a pointed cone shape.

2 Make a spine by pinching the pointed end between your thumb and finger.

3 Roll a green ball for the head; make 2 eye indentations. Roll 2 small white balls, and add pupils. Roll a small green ball for the nose. Make a smile with a size 2 piping tip.

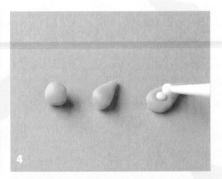

4 For the ears, roll 2 green balls; shape into cones. Push a small blue ball into the wide end of each using a ball modeling tool.

5 Glue the ears to the head and add the eyes and nose. Add a thin curl of light-blue fondant to make the hair.

CAKE DESIGN

For a really great effect, make a set of these monsters in all the colors of the rainbow and place each one on a cupcake with matching buttercream. In the design shown here, I have created a landscape based on rock and dry land. You can create this landscape on a board around a large cake or on the cake itself.

Bertie

THE ALIEN

You can make this character any size you choose. For the size shown here, use the templates on page 185. The fondant colors for Bertie are blue, white, green, black, pink, and yellow. For the accessories, you will need gray fondant.

YOU WILL NEED:
- Basic modeling kit
  (*see pages 12–13*)
- Fondant (blue, white, green, black, pink, yellow, gray)
- 30-gauge white floral wire
- Lilac and snowflake luster dust
- Black, gray, and white edible dusting powder
- Toothbrush

Using blue fondant, roll a large ball for the body and a smaller one for the head.

Roll the larger ball into a cone shape. Use your thumb to press down on the front to make a big, round belly.

Add a belly button using a needle tool or toothpick.

To make a tail, roll a blue ball into a long cone shape and press the fatter end to flatten it.

Glue the flat section of the tail underneath the bottom. Push 1 or 2 lengths of spaghetti into the body, right to the base.

Shape the head ball into an oval and push it onto the body so the spaghetti is completely covered.

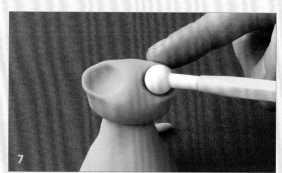

Use a large ball modeling tool to make eye sockets. Create a thin rim around each eye by pressing the fondant against your finger with the ball tool.

Using a scalpel, cut a groove into the fondant to make a gently smiling mouth.

For the eyes, roll 2 white balls and cut in half. Use your fingertips to soften the cut sides. The eyes should be slightly oval.

TOP TIP
When making large eyes, always roll a ball or an oval and cut it in half. Only use the front half of the ball; otherwise, the eyes will protrude too much. If this does occur, slice a little off the back and reshape.

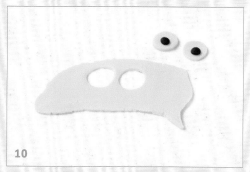

Roll out some green fondant and cut out 2 circles (smaller than the white pieces). Glue them onto the white fondant (*see Top Tip, left*).

Make a small indentation in each green circle and glue on 2 tiny black balls to make pupils.

12 Glue the completed eyes into the sockets.

13 Roll a small ball of pink fondant to make a nose.

14 Using yellow fondant, roll some small balls and press them onto the body so they are flat. Use your flat-ended color shaper to smooth out the edges and hide the joins.

TOP TIP
When adding fondant spots, roll or press them so that they are very thin before applying them to the body. Use a flat-ended color shaper to blend the joins so the spots appear seamless.

15 Glue 2 tiny blue balls to the top of the head, ready to insert the antennae.

16 To make the feet, roll 2 blue balls. Using the side of your thumb, press 1 half of each ball to flatten.

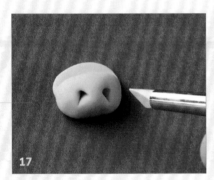

17 Insert the angle chisel color shaper into the front of each foot as shown, to create claws.

18 Attach the feet by applying glue to the flattened surface of each foot and positioning underneath the body.

TOP TIP
When making aliens, try to exaggerate some of their features by making them unusually large. Here I have given Bertie extra-long arms and big eyes. This helps to make him look particularly alien-like, and not like any other character.

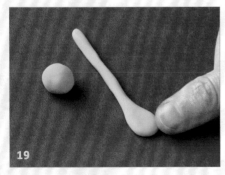

19 For the arms, roll 2 blue balls. Shape 1 ball into a sausage (longer than the body) with a ball at one end. Press the ball flat.

20 The flattened ball will be the hand. Cut out a piece of fondant to make a thumb, then shorten the thumb.

21 Using your thumb and finger, soften the edges of the thumb and the rest of the hand.

22

Repeat steps 19–21 to make the other arm, then glue both arms in place.

23

At this point, your alien should look like this.

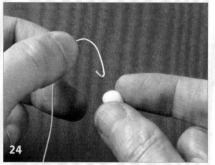

24

To make the antennae, push a small ball of fondant onto a piece of 30-gauge floral wire (this is very easy to bend).

TOP TIP
Don't use wire if you're making a children's cake—it isn't edible. If you want the alien to be fully edible, replace the wire with licorice strings, rice noodles, or anything edible and bendy.

25

Cover the balls in lilac and snowflake luster dust.

26

Dip the ends of the wire in edible glue, then push them into the head, through the small balls you attached in step 24.

27

Your finished alien should look like this.

TOP TIP
Remember the key rule: the bigger the eyes, the cuter the character— this doesn't just apply to babies. Big eyes are perceived as cute all over the world.

Planet

1 Roll out some sausages of fondant and place them in a circle on the top of a cake or cake board to make a crater.

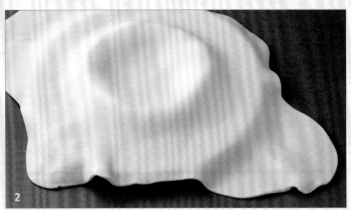

2 Roll out some gray fondant and lay it over the entire cake or board.

3 Make dents in the fondant using your ball modeling tool.

4 Make edible paint in black, gray, and white (*see page 9*). With a toothbrush, flick the paint over the fondant using black, then gray, then a little white.

TOP TIP
When flicking color with a toothbrush, always make sure your table, walls, and floor are well covered in case you flick paint in the wrong direction.

CAKE DESIGN
An alien that looks cute and vulnerable is best left as a solitary figure on a cake. For the picture opposite, I used a round 12-inch (30-cm) cake with a large surface area to make Bertie look a little lost and lonely on his own planet.

GoOba

THE ALIEN

You can make this character any size you choose. For the size shown here, use the templates on page 184. The fondant colors for Gooba are green, white, pink, black, and blue. For the accessories, you will need red fondant.

YOU WILL NEED:
- Basic modeling kit (*see pages 12–13*)
- Fondant (green, white, pink, black, blue, and red)
- Red and pink edible dusting powder
- Snowflake luster dust

Roll a large green ball for the body and a smaller one for the head.

Roll the larger ball into a cone shape.

Insert a piece of spaghetti into the body, right to the base, and make a belly button using a needle tool.

TOP TIP
A novelty character is almost always made cuter by the addition of a belly button.

Roll the smaller ball into an egg shape to make the head.

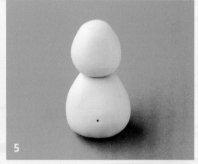

Place the head on the body so that the spaghetti is completely covered.

Make eye sockets using a ball modeling tool. To make a rim around each eye, use the tool to press the fondant against your finger. Ensure the sockets are the same shape.

Make a defined brow using a flat-ended color shaper.

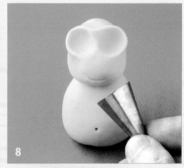

Use a size 2 piping tip to make a mouth.

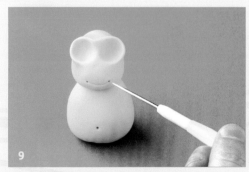

Define the ends of the mouth by adding dimples with a needle tool.

Roll 2 balls of white fondant and cut them in half so that they each have a flat base.

Glue the eyes into the sockets.

12 Roll out some pink fondant and cut out 2 small circles. Glue them onto the eyes, and add 2 tiny black balls to make the pupils.

TOP TIP
To further exaggerate the cuteness of big eyes, make them look up toward the recipient of the cake instead of facing forward.

13 At this stage, your alien should look like this.

14 Roll a green cone and bend the pointed end. Make an dent in the round end with a ball modeling tool.

15 Fill the dent with a small ball of blue fondant; then glue in place and press flat.

16 Repeat steps 14–15 to make the second ear; then glue both ears in place.

17 Your alien should look like this.

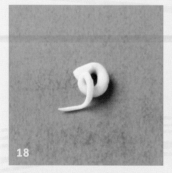

18 Roll out a sausage of blue fondant and twist into a curl.

19 Glue the curl on top of the head.

20 To make the feet, roll 2 balls of green fondant. Form 1 ball into a long cone shape, leaving a large part of the ball at one end.

21 Pinch the ball to make a flat foot shape. Make the foot as large as you can without making it too thin.

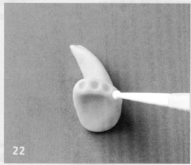

22 At the end of the foot, make 4 indentations with a small ball modeling tool to form toes.

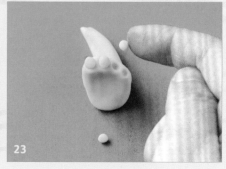

23 Glue a tiny green ball into each indentation; the balls should decrease slightly in size as you work along the foot.

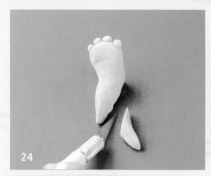

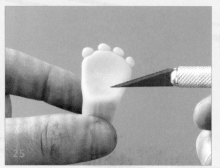

Cut off the pointed end of the leg so that it isn't too long.

Make slight creases in the foot using a scalpel.

Repeat steps 20–25 to make the second leg, then attach both legs to the body using edible glue.

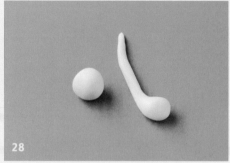

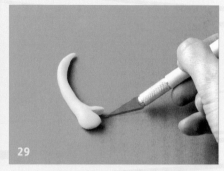

Your alien should now look like this.

To make the arms, roll 2 green balls into long sausages with a ball shape at one end.

Take 1 arm and press the ball end to flatten; this will make the hand. With a scalpel, cut a piece out of the hand to make a thumb.

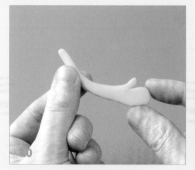

Use your finger and thumb to soften the edges of the thumb and the hand.

Gently push the thumb toward the hand.

Repeat steps 29–31 to make the other arm. Attach the arms to the body using edible glue.

Your finished alien should look like this.

Eugene the alien

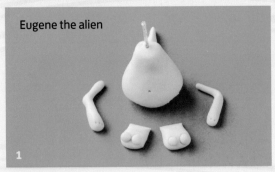

1 For Gooba's friend, make the body, 2 feet, and arms as shown. Use the techniques applied to Gooba on pages 107–109.

2 Make the head in the same way you made Gooba's head.

3 Attach the head to the body and glue in place.

Radar the alien

1 Make the head using the principles applied to Gooba, but give Radar a slightly longer head. Attach to the back of a crater on the cake or board. The hands are made in the same way as for Gooba (*see steps 29–31*).

Landscape

1 Cover your cake or board with a ring of fondant, making it higher at the back than at the front.

2 Brush your cake or board with cooled boiled water, and cover in red fondant. Using a wheel tool, draw lines over the fondant as shown.

3 To make paint, mix red, pink, and white edible dusts with dipping solution (*see page 9*). Paint the fondant with color streaks for texture.

CAKE DESIGN
In the image shown opposite, I have used a cake board to display Gooba and his friends. This line design would work perfectly on a tall cake or small cupcakes. Make sure you allow the lines to follow the natural shape of the cake.

TROPICAL CREATURES

ROXY

THE OCTOPUS

You can make this character any size you choose. For the size shown here, use the templates on page 186. The fondant colors for Roxy are pink, white, purple, and black. For the accessories, you will need blue, gray, pink, white, and black fondant, and green gum paste.

YOU WILL NEED:
- Basic modeling kit (see pages 12–13)
- Fondant (pink, white, purple, black, blue, and gray)
- Pink edible dusting powder
- Blue royal icing
- Piping bag
- Gray and snowflake luster dust
- Shell molds
- Lime green gum paste
- Leaf cutter
- Foam mat

1

Roll a large ball of pink fondant for the body.

2

Cut out 2 white ovals using a cutter about ¾ inch (2 cm) long and 2 purple ovals with a cutter about ⅝ inch (1.5 cm) long.

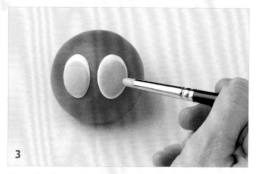

3

To make the eyes, glue the ovals onto the body as shown, and use a flat-ended color shaper to create a seamless join.

4

Cut out 2 black fondant circles half the size of the purple ovals, and glue on tiny white fondant balls.

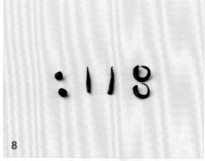

5

Glue the black circles in place as shown.

6

To make the mouth, roll out a pink fondant sausage and bend it slightly. Push the wide end of a size 2 piping tip into the fondant to make a smile.

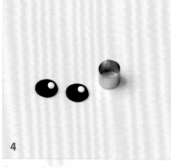

7

Glue the mouth in place, then dust the smile with pink edible dusting powder.

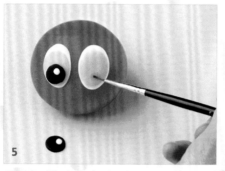

8

To make the eyelashes, roll out 4 balls of black fondant into cones, then curl as shown.

9

Glue 2 eyelashes above each eye.

TOP TIP

If you have a character that needs to be assembled on a cake, ensure that you plan ahead and ice your cake at least one day before you want to add the character. Otherwise, the fondant on the cake will be too soft and will dent when touched.

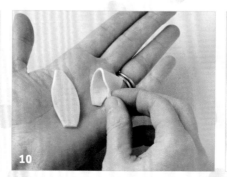

10

To make the bow, cut 2 pieces of fondant into lozenge shapes. Fold over each piece and glue the ends together.

11

If you accidentally squash the bow, reopen using a ball modeling tool.

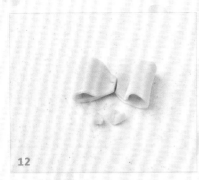

12

Cut off the tip of each piece using a scalpel, then glue the 2 halves of the bow together.

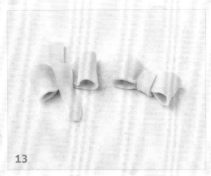

13

Cut out a strip of fondant and wrap it around the join. Cut to size and glue the end underneath the bow.

14

Glue the bow onto the head and dust lightly with pink edible dusting powder. (If you want to dust the creases of the bow, do so before attaching it to the head.)

15

Roxy needs to be assembled on the cake; cover your cake with light-blue fondant now. Cut long, wavy strips in dark-blue fondant and glue around the sides.

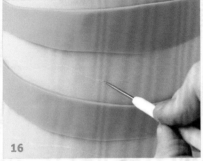

16

Using a pin tool, scratch lines onto the cake—these will guide you as you pipe the dots in the next step.

17

Put some blue royal icing into a piping bag, and pipe dots along the scratched lines.

18

Stop after every 15–20 dots and gently use a damp brush to push down any peaks on your dots so they are all nicely rounded.

19

To make each leg, roll out a ball of fondant into a cone about 6 inches (15 cm) long. Indent the wider end with your thumb.

20

Cover the leg with light-pink balls, squashing them flat as you glue them on.

TOP TIP

Children don't mind if you use unrealistic colors, so have fun playing with your color palette. As long as you give the character key features—like 8 legs for an octopus—your character will be recognizable.

21

Curl the leg into a twisted shape.

22

Glue the leg onto the cake. To ensure all the legs are the same distance from the middle, mark the center with a dot of paste.

23

Make another 7 legs, and glue them in place around the center dot. You can then glue on the body, or if you want it to sit higher, add a ring of fondant as shown.

24

Your finished octopus should look like this.

Benji the Clam

1

Roll a ball of light-gray fondant about 1½ inches (4 cm) in diameter.

2

Cut the ball in half.

Pinch the edges of the cut side of each half, to make them soft and wavy.

4

With a small ball modeling tool, make 2 indentations for eyes. Gently mark both halves of the fondant all over the surface with a shell pattern.

5

To make a tongue, cut out a pink semicircle and mark a crease down the middle. Glue in place as shown.

TOP TIP

Whenever you are piping with royal icing, always have a small brush and a bowl of water nearby. Even the best pipers will occasionally have little peaks in their piping. These can be smoothed out by tapping them gently with a damp brush.

6

Glue the 2 halves of the clam together along 1 side. (If the mouth won't stay open, place a piece of fondant at the back of the tongue.) Glue a length of white fondant around the mouth.

7

Glue on 2 white fondant balls for eyes, then add smaller black fondant pupils. Dust the clam with gray and snowflake luster dust.

Pearls and shells

1

Using a variety of shell molds and white fondant or gum paste, make a selection of shell shapes (*see Top Tip, right*).

2

Dust the shells with snowflake luster dust. To make pearls, roll fondant balls through the dust. Decorate the cake with shells and pearls.

TOP TIP

When using a mold, make sure no fondant or paste is hanging over the edge of the mold before removing the fondant.

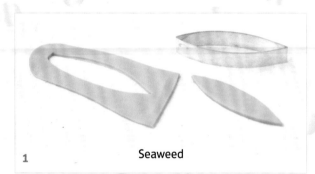

1 Seaweed

To make the seaweed, color some gum paste in lime green and cut out some long leaf shapes.

2

On a foam mat, press the edges of the leaf with a ball modeling tool to give a wave effect, then glue in place on the sides of the cake.

CAKE DESIGN

When making an octopus, whether on a large cake or a cupcake, it's usually best to assemble the character on the cake as you go along. Ensure you have prepared the size of your cake to fit your octopus. Here, I used a cake about 6 inches (15 cm) round and 7 inches (18 cm) high. For cupcakes, make the cakes first and assemble the octopuses on the top so the legs can hang off the side.

BOOMER
THE FISH

YOU WILL NEED:
- Basic modeling kit (*see pages 12–13*)
- Fondant (yellow, white, blue, black, and red)
- Red, orange, and yellow edible dusting powder
- Black edible color marker
- Dark modeling chocolate
- 18-gauge floral wire
- Cotton thread
- Black gum paste

You can make this character any size you choose. For the size shown here, use the templates on page 187. The fondant colors for the fish are yellow, white, blue, and black. For the accessories, you will need red, blue, and white fondant, brown modeling chocolate, and black gum paste.

1

Roll a large ball of yellow fondant for the body.

2

Roll the ball into a cone shape.

3

To create a ridge along the center of the cone, pinch the fondant between your index fingers.

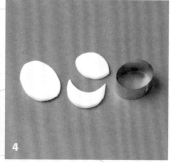

4

Cut out a white fondant shape with an oval cutter 1½ inches (4 cm) long. Remove a section to make a crescent.

5

Glue the crescent onto the yellow fondant as shown, for the teeth.

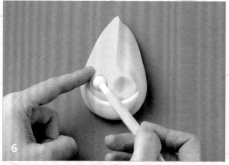

6

Push a ball modeling tool into the fondant, pressing against your finger to make eye sockets.

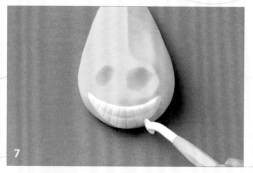

7

Use a wheel tool to draw on the teeth as shown.

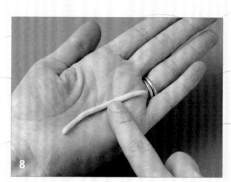

8

Roll out a length of yellow fondant, then cut it in half.

9

Glue one half around the top of the mouth and the other around the bottom.

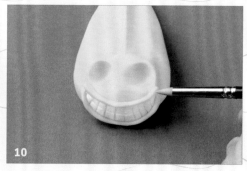

10

Where the 2 pieces meet, smooth out the seam using a pointed color shaper.

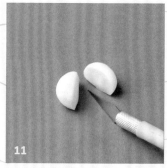

11

To make the eyes, roll a ½-inch (1-cm) ball of white fondant and cut it in half.

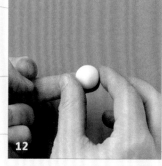

12

Pinch around the edge of each half so that they each have a round top and a flat base.

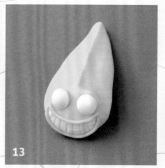

13

Glue the eyes in position in the sockets (rounded sides facing up).

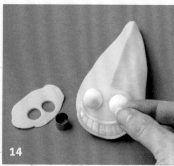

14

Roll out some light-blue fondant, cut out 2 small circles, then glue them onto the white eyes.

15

Glue 2 small black fondant pupils onto the blue circles.

16

To make the eyelids, cut out 2 yellow circles, then cut out a crescent shape from each circle as shown.

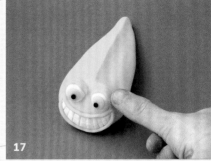

17

Glue the crescent shapes around the eyes, tucking in the points at the sides.

18

Gently press a flat-ended color shaper around each eyelid, about a fingernail width from the back edge, to create a rim.

19

For the top fin, roll out a sausage of yellow fondant and flatten into a harp shape. As you press the fondant between your fingers, the edges will become wavy.

20

For the tail fin, pinch a ball into a teardrop shape with wavy edges.

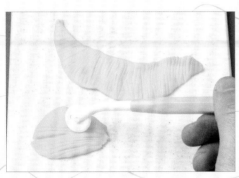

Draw lines over the surfaces of both fins using a wheel tool. Go over the same area several times so that the edges tear a little.

22

Add a line of glue along the ridge created in step 3, then glue on the top fin.

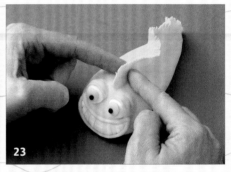

23

Secure the fin in place by pinching with your fingertips.

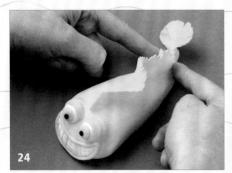

24

Glue on the tail fin in the same way.

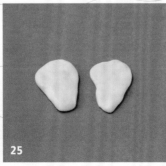

25

To make the side fins, roll 2 balls of yellow fondant and press flat to create teardrop shapes.

26

Roll over both sides of each piece with a wheel tool, again allowing the fondant to tear at the edges.

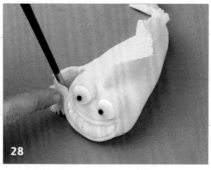

TOP TIP
When you're making an animal that isn't particularly attractive, such as a fish or a turtle, aim to make it cute and impish so that the recipient finds it hard to resist. Big eyes always make a character look very cute.

27
Take 1 of the fins, and glue the tip in place at the side of the fish.

28
Bend the fin around a brush or thin stick, and glue the other end to the fish as shown.

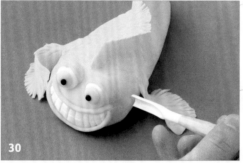

29
Take the second fin, and glue the tip in place on the other side of the fish. Let it flap out to the side.

30
Mark the entire body with scales, using a smile tool as shown. Work from the face back to the tail.

31
Dust red, orange, and yellow edible dusting powders over the body.

32
Dust the fin along the base with slightly darker red and orange tints.

TOP TIP
For certain characters you may want to have a blended color. You can do this using edible dusting powders. Here, rather than make the fish orange, I have used yellow and then dusted in reds, oranges, and yellows. This gives a more realistic and interesting look to the fish.

33
Your finished fish should look like this.

Willie the Worm

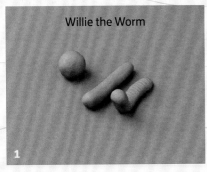

1

Roll a ball of pale red fondant, and shape it into a sausage. Turn up one end to create a head.

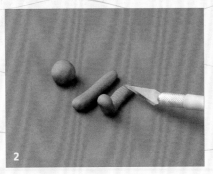

2

Mark lines along the back of the worm using a scalpel.

3

Draw on a face with black edible ink, and, if you wish, add little sausage shapes to some of the worms to make arms.

Fishing rod

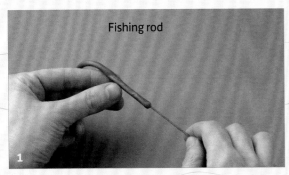

1

Roll a thin sausage of dark modeling chocolate, and insert a length of 18-gauge wire. (To make the rod edible, use spaghetti rather than wire and make the sausage thicker.)

2

As you push in the wire, the chocolate will bunch up, so roll out the chocolate with the wire inside on a board.

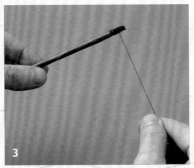

3

Wrap some cotton around the end of the chocolate.

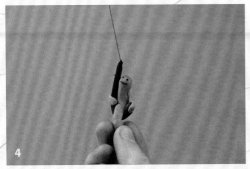

4

Make a small hook from black gum paste; then twist the thread onto the hook. Allow the hook to dry; then glue a worm in place and add arms.

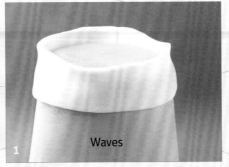

1

Waves

Cover your cake with blue fondant. Glue a wavy strip of white fondant around the cake, letting it sit higher than the top of the cake.

2

Add a layer of glue around the base of, and underneath, the first strip.

3

Place another fondant strip over the glue. You can use a second white piece, or, for a smaller cake, start grading into light blue.

4

Continue to add more strips in the same way, until you reach the base. Make each strip a little darker than the last by adding color to the fondant.

CAKE DESIGN

A fish has no limbs, so consider how he'll fit into your design. I made a tall cake using two 6-inch (15-cm) cakes and one 4-inch (10-cm) cake. I cut, leveled, and stacked the cakes; then I carved them to make sloped sides. I then covered the cakes. The "waves" technique can also be used for grass, sand, and fire.

TONTO

THE TURTLE

YOU WILL NEED:
- Basic modeling kit
  (*see pages 12–13*)
- Fondant (green, white, blue,
  black, and various other colors)
- Edible dusting powders in
  various greens and bright colors
- Gum paste in various colors
  including white and green
- Shell molds
- Snowflake luster dust

You can make this character any size you choose. For the size shown here, use the templates on page 186. The fondant colors for the turtle are green, white, blue, and black. For the accessories, you will need pink, yellow, green, blue, and red fondant, and white and green gum paste.

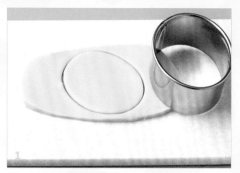

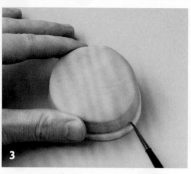

Roll out light-green fondant about ⅛ inch (3 mm) thick. Cut out an oval about 2¾ inches (7 cm) long.

Roll out darker-green fondant about ½ inch (1 cm) thick, and cut out an oval the same size as in step 1.

Glue the darker-green oval onto the lighter one.

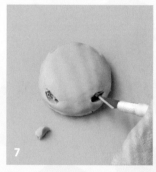

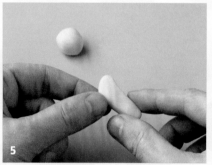

Use your fingers to curve the edges of the fondant—like a shell. It doesn't need to be perfect since it won't be seen.

To make the back flippers, roll 2 light-green fondant balls, and pinch them flat, curving them slightly at the ends.

To make the front flippers, pinch 2 light-green balls into long, flat cones.

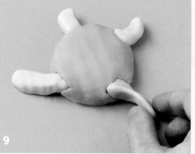

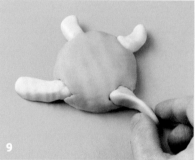

TOP TIP
When you make a turtle, try to make one flipper twisted to give the illusion of movement.

Using a scalpel, make 4 cuts in the dark-green oval, ready to insert the flippers.

Put some glue into each of the slits.

Put the flippers into the slits. Twist 1 front flipper up so you can slip a small shell underneath it later.

Roll out some more dark-green fondant, and cut out a larger oval about 3 inches (8 cm) long.

Rest the oval over the body. If it's too small, gently pull it to stretch it a little.

Glue the fondant onto the body to create the shell. It should be wrapped around the arms so they appear to be pushing out from underneath.

13

Cut out a section at the front of the body using a round cutter. This is where the neck will go.

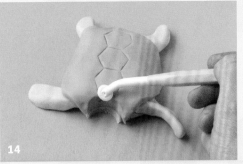

14

Using a wheel tool, draw hexagon shapes all over the shell (they don't need to be perfect).

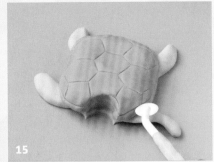

15

Draw a line around the edge of the shell, about 1/8 inch (3 mm) up from the base.

16

Dust the shell with edible dusting powder in different shades of green. Apply randomly for a more realistic look.

17

Mix the darkest-green powder you've used with dipping solution, and, using a size 1 paintbrush, paint in the hexagonal lines.

18

Paint light-green spots on the arms and legs.

19

Outline the spots in a darker green.

TOP TIP
A turtle's neck should always appear as if it is stretching out of the shell. This is a key characteristic of a turtle.

20

At this stage, your turtle should look like this. Make sure the flippers are now secure.

21

To make the neck, roll a ball of light-green fondant into a cone.

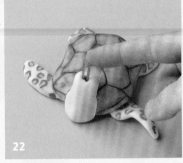

22

Glue the neck into the space you cut out of the body, then insert 2 lengths of spaghetti as shown.

23

Roll a ball of light-green fondant for the head.

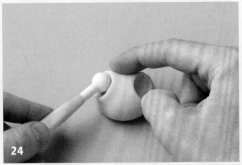

24

To make the eye sockets, push a large ball modeling tool into the fondant, and press it against your finger.

25

To make rims around the eye sockets, gently push around the eye line with a flat-ended color shaper as shown.

26 Paint the head with spots in the same way as you did the arms and legs; then make a smile using a size 2 piping tip.

27 Push the head onto the pieces of spaghetti and glue in place.

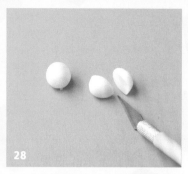

28 To make eyes, cut a ½-inch (1-cm) ball of white fondant into 2 halves.

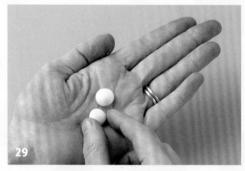

29 Pinch around the flat side of each semicircle to define the edges.

31 Glue the eyes into the sockets to complete your turtle. Your finished turtle should look like this.

30 Glue 2 blue fondant circles to the whites of the eyes; then glue on 2 black circles and, finally, tiny white pupils.

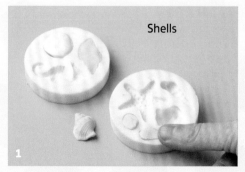

1 Press gum paste (or a mixture of half gum paste and half fondant) into a shell mold. Ensure you can see the outlines, then remove.

Shells

2 Make shells in pink, lemon yellow, light green, and light blue.

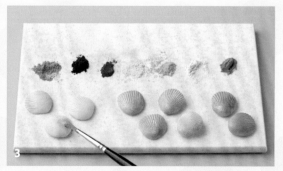

3 Dust the shells with edible dusting powders, using a rainbow of colors.

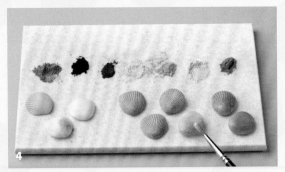

Add snowflake luster dust to the shells to make them shimmer.

Make green shells using a mixture of red and green tints, then add snowflake luster dust. The red will disappear as it blends in.

You should now have a selection of shells in different colors and shapes.

Corals

To make sponges, roll different-colored balls of fondant. To achieve this pattern, push in a small ball modeling tool all over the surface.

For the pattern shown above, roll a wheel tool all over the surface.

The pattern shown here is made by snipping the fondant with the tip of a pair of scissors.

TOP TIP
When making abstract patterns on sea fauna, use household objects like a sponge, fabric, a fork, or lace to create different effects.

Using any color, roll a ball of fondant into a cone and push a large ball modeling tool into the wider end. Make several of these corals to group together.

If you want to pattern them more, use a wheel tool to draw lines around the rim.

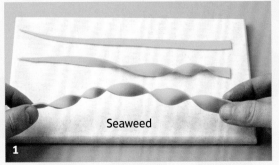

CAKE DESIGN
For the picture opposite, I baked a 7-inch (18-cm) round cake that was 4 inches (10 cm) high. The seaweed is pushed into the fondant on the cake and the corals. Any joins are covered by shells and fauna. Tropical marine life is very colorful so use lots of color in the shells around the cake.

Roll out some gum paste and make holes with a piping tip and a round cutter. Bend into shape. Leave to dry for at least 2 hours.

Seaweed

Roll out some green gum paste and cut out long, thin triangles. Hold each one at both ends and twist. Leave to dry for at least 24 hours, ideally 48 hours.

CHARLIE

THE PARROT

YOU WILL NEED:
- Basic modeling kit (*see pages 12–13*)
- Fondant (green, yellow, white, blue, black, and pink)
- Bubble (boba) tea straw
- 18-gauge floral wire
- Brown floral tape
- Modeling chocolate
- Primrose cutter set
- White and green gum paste
- Purple luster dust
- Snowflake, green, brown, and cream edible dusting powders
- Variety of large petal cutters
- White stamens

You can make this character any size you choose. For the size shown here, use the templates on page 187. The fondant colors for the parrot are green, yellow, white, blue, and black. For the accessories, you will need white, pink, and light green fondant. You will also need white and green gum paste.

1

Roll a ball of light-green fondant for the body.

2

Roll part of the ball into a neck shape as shown, keeping the rounded section at the base fairly large.

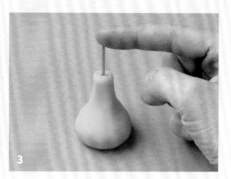

3

Push a length of spaghetti into the fondant, right to the base.

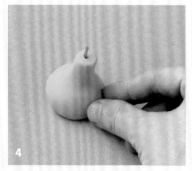

4

Pinch the fondant on one side so that you have a slightly pointed area to attach the tail feathers to.

5

To make the wings, roll 2 balls of green fondant, and shape them into cones.

6

Flatten 1 cone between your thumb and finger.

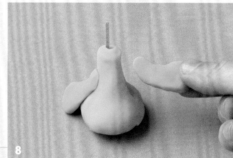

7

Glue the first wing in place as shown.

8

Repeat steps 6–7 to make the second wing.

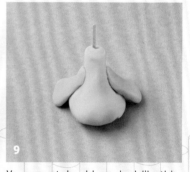

9

Your parrot should now look like this.

10

To make the wing feathers, roll small balls of darker-green fondant and press each one flat.

11

Pinch the end of each piece to make feather shapes.

TOP TIP
Parrots look good in many different colors, but they are most effective if you stick to red, blue, yellow, or green. The principles used for this parrot also apply to making a toucan.

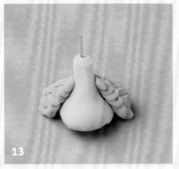

Cover the wings with the feathers, starting at the back and the bottom of each wing and overlapping the feathers.

Your parrot wings should look like this.

Next, your parrot needs a branch to sit on. Push a bubble tea straw into your cake and cut it to the height of the cake.

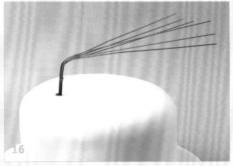

TOP TIP
For food-safety reasons, floral wire must never come into contact with your cake. If you are intending to put wire into your cake, either put a flower pick into the cake and sit the wire in the pick, or, as shown here, cover the wire with floral tape, then put it into a bubble tea straw (or other wide drinking straw).

Group together 6–8 lengths of 18-gauge floral wire; then wrap with brown floral tape to about 1¼ inches (3 cm) higher than the cake.

Insert the wire into the straw, then bend to form a right angle about 1¼ inches (3 cm) above the cake height.

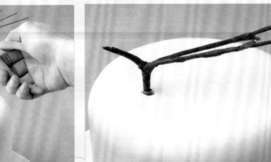

Cut the wires using wire cutters; then bend them to make 2 main branches and a couple of twigs (do this by bending the tips of the wires).

Wrap brown floral tape around the wires as shown.

Cover the wires with dark modeling chocolate.

Smooth the chocolate between your thumb and finger. The tape underneath will give it a realistic bumpy effect.

Dip a pointed color shaper in water and use it to smooth any remaining unwanted bumps in the chocolate.

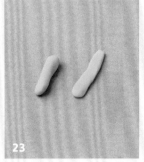

22

Sit your parrot in the tree so that it perches between the branches. You can glue it in place if you wish.

23

To make the tail feathers, roll 3 long dark green cones, and press flat.

24

Glue the tail feathers in place on the back of the parrot.

25

To make the feet, using yellow fondant, roll out 2 crescent shapes, and mark 2 lines on each one with a stitching tool.

26

Glue the feet to the branch at the front of the parrot's body.

27

To make the head, roll a ball of green fondant, and make it slightly egg-shaped (not too pointed).

28

Make 2 indentations with a ball modeling tool for the eye sockets. Cut out an oval piece to make a hole for the beak to slot into.

29

Make some head feathers by rolling out little cones of green fondant and using any spare wing feathers.

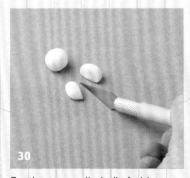

30

For the eyes, roll a ball of white fondant, and cut it in half.

31

Smooth down the 2 halves so that they are round on top and flat underneath.

32

Glue a circle of light-blue fondant to each eye, then make an indentation in each one, ready for the pupils.

33 Roll 2 tiny balls of black fondant for pupils and glue them into the indentations. Glue the eyes into the sockets.

34 To make eyelids, roll out 2 thin green sausages, and bend into arches. Glue in place to cover the tops of the eyes.

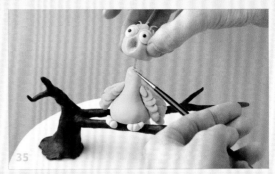

35 Glue the head onto the body.

36 Make sure you are happy with the direction in which the head is facing.

37 To make the beak, roll a ball of yellow fondant, and gently flatten it. Make a line as shown. (*See Top Tip, right.*)

TOP TIP
The beak is tricky to get right the first time. Always measure the ball of yellow fondant against the face to make sure it isn't too big or too small.

38 Cut out a section to make a mouth.

39 Cut away the back of the fondant with a round cutter.

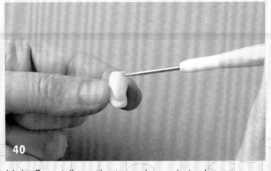

40 Make 2 nostrils on the top using a pin tool.

TOP TIP
Allow the beak to harden a little before gluing it in place. This way, you won't squash it if you press too hard.

41 Glue the beak into the hollow made in step 28 (*see Top Tip, left*).

42 Check that the beak looks correct from the side.

TOP TIP
You don't have to balance your parrot on a branch. If he is on the cake instead, just flip his tail feathers out so that they're horizontal instead of vertical. If placing him on the tree, put him between 2 branches. By putting his feet on the front branch only, it will look like he is balancing on that branch.

Also check that the beak doesn't look too big from the front. Your finished parrot should look like this.

Small flowers

To make the flowers, roll out some white gum paste and cut out some small petals. Leave to dry in a foam flower tray—they will naturally curl. Paint with purple and snowflake luster dust.

Leaves

To make the leaves, roll out some light-green gum paste and cut out leaf shapes in various sizes. Cut out triangular pieces from along the edges as shown, then mark out the veins with a wheel tool.

Bend the leaves and allow to dry for at least 2 hours (ideally 24 hours); then dust with green edible dusting powder. You can also make tiny leaves to sit on the tree. Glue any leaves to the tree.

Tropical Creatures   **137**

Bamboo

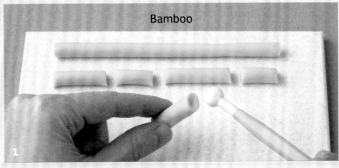

Roll out a sausage of light-green fondant about ⅜ inch (8 mm) wide; then cut into pieces of varying length. Push a large ball modeling tool into both ends of each piece.

Dust the bamboo with a mixture of green, brown, and cream edible dusting powders.

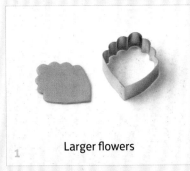

Larger flowers

Choose any petal cutter and cut out 5 or 6 petals from gum paste.

Use a ball modeling tool to give the petals wavy edges.

Leave the petals to dry in a foam flower tray for at least 2 hours—ideally 24 hours.

Roll a ball of fondant and glue the petals around it as shown. (Some flowers require 5 petals and others 6 petals.)

Roll a ball of fondant and push in the stamens. (These are not edible, so leave them out if you prefer.)

Glue the flower center into the middle of the flower.

CAKE DESIGN

For the design opposite, I used an 8-inch (20-cm) round cake that was 4½ inches (12 cm) high and covered it in cream fondant. I put the bamboo around the sides and decorated the branches and the cake with tropical-looking flowers.

Farm Animals

Debbie
THE DUCK

You can make this character any size you choose. For the size shown here, use the templates on page 188. The fondant colors for the duck are yellow, orange, white, and black. For the accessories, you will need yellow and brown fondant, and green, pink, and white gum paste.

Roll 2 balls of yellow fondant for the body and the head.

Shape the larger ball into a cone. Lengthen the pointed end to make the neck, and keep the wider end rounded to make a big bottom.

Push a length of spaghetti (or 2 if needed) downward into the fondant to make a support as shown.

Using your thumb and finger, pinch the bottom to form a more pointed tail.

Take the smaller ball and roll one end in the palm of your hand to make the top of the head.

TOP TIP
To make your characters appear friendly and cute, always make the "brain" end of the head smaller than the mouth end.

The head should be shaped as shown here.

Position the head on top of the neck (do not glue).

Roll out some orange fondant and use a ⅝-inch (1.5-cm) teardrop cutter to cut out 2 shapes. These will make the feet.

Using the end of a drinking straw, cut out semicircles along the rounded end of each foot.

Using the back of a scalpel, mark 3 lines along each foot to indicate webbing.

Cut off the pointed end of each foot.

12

Glue the feet in place underneath the body of the duck.

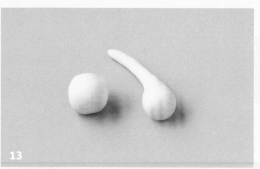

13

To make the arms, roll 2 balls of yellow fondant. Roll 1 end of each ball into a thin sausage.

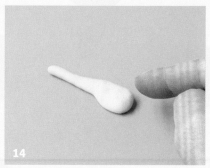

14

Take 1 wing and flatten the ball-shaped end with your fingertip.

15

Using a scalpel, cut 4 long, thin triangles out of the flattened end to make 5 fingers.

16

Gently pinch each finger to make a gently curved shape.

17

Repeat steps 14–16 to make the other arm, then glue both arms to the body (it's easier if you remove the head first).

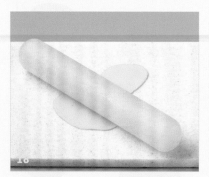

18

To make the hair, roll out a piece of yellow fondant very thinly.

19

Cut out a small irregular star shape with 6 or 7 points.

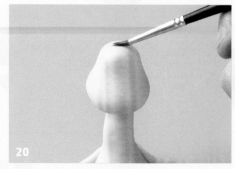

20

Glue the star shape onto the head with edible glue to make the hair.

21

Turn up the ends of the hair using your fingertip.

22

To make the beak, roll a ball of orange fondant into a cone shape.

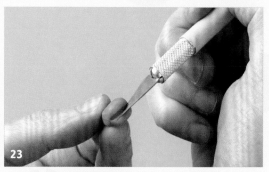

23

Hold the beak between your fingertips and cut a slit in the round end to make the mouth.

24

Cut off the point of the cone.

25

Add 2 nostrils using a needle tool.

26

Glue the beak in position, making sure it's two-thirds of the way down the face, covering both the mouth and the nose area.

27

For the eyes, roll 2 white balls of fondant and glue in place, then add 2 tiny balls of black fondant to make the pupils.

TOP TIP

To make hair for animals, roll out some fondant very thinly and cut out a star shape. Then turn up the points using your fingertips or a toothpick.

28

Your finished duck should look like this.

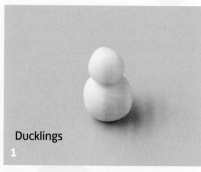

Ducklings

1

Roll 2 small balls of yellow fondant to make a body and a head. Glue the smaller ball on top of the larger one.

2

To make the feet, repeat the method used for the duck (steps 8–11), but use a smaller cutter. For the wings, squash 2 yellow balls into flat wing shapes.

3

Glue the wings and feet in place.

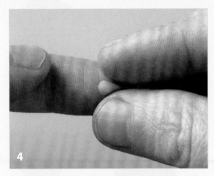

4

To make a tiny beak, roll a small orange ball. Shape the tip into a point using your thumb and fingertips as shown.

5

Add little black fondant eyes to complete your duckling; alternatively, use black nonpareils. Repeat steps 1–5 to make more ducklings.

1 Lily pad

Cut out a circle of green gum paste or fondant, and cut out a section as shown.

2

Roll a veining tool over the surface to create a lily-pad texture.

3

Dust the edges of the lily pad with dark-green edible dusting powder.

1 Pink flowers

Roll out some pink and white gum paste and cut out flower shapes using sunflower, daisy, and gerbera cutters.

2

Leave to dry in a foil tray or flower former for at least 2 hours—ideally 24 hours.

3

Roll a ball of yellow fondant for each flower. Prick them all over with a needle tool.

4

Glue each yellow ball into the center of a flower.

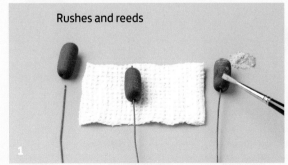

1 Rushes and reeds

Cut lengths of floral wire and dip in glue. Push each into a brown fondant sausage; roll over a waffle weave dish towel to emboss. Dust with edible light cream or buttermilk tint.

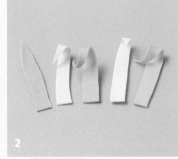

2

For reeds, cut long, thin triangles of green gum paste and curl the tips. Leave to dry for 24 hours.

CAKE DESIGN

For the design opposite, I used a cake around 8 inches round and 4½ inches high (20 cm x 12 cm). The cake is covered in blue fondant, and the flowers are added to the top with scattered ducklings. The sides of the cake are decorated with reeds and rushes. You could also paint water ripples onto the blue fondant using gel paste food coloring mixed with water.

Coco

THE COW

YOU WILL NEED:
- Basic modeling kit
  (*see pages 12–13*)
- Fondant (white, black, pink, and green)
- Small heart plunger cutter
- Small blossom plunger cutter
- Cake smoother

You can make this character any size you choose. For the size shown here, use the templates on page 189. The fondant colors for Coco are white, black, pink, and green. You will need the same colors for the accessories.

1

Roll 2 balls of white fondant for the body and the head.

2

Roll the larger ball into a wide-based cone shape.

3

Push a length of spaghetti down into the fondant to make a support as shown.

4

Roll the smaller ball into an egg shape.

5

Position the head on the spaghetti to check that the head is in proportion with the body.

6

To make the patch on the body, roll a ball of black fondant and press flat. Pinch the edges to make an irregular shape.

7

Glue the patch onto the body, and soften the edges using a flat-ended color shaper.

8

Roll out some light-pink fondant, and cut an oval shape about the same size as the wider end of the head.

9

Gently pinch the edges flat.

10

Place the head on the body, and glue the oval to the face. Flatten the edges using a flat-ended color shaper to make a seamless join.

11

Using the small end of a ball modeling tool, make 2 indentations for the nostrils.

TOP TIP
When working with black and white, make all the white parts together, then all the black parts. Black fondant will always leave a residue on your hands, so wash them before moving on to the next stage so you don't turn your white fondant gray.

12

Gently push the wide end of a size 2 piping tip into the pink fondant to make a smile.

13

Using a needle tool, make 2 holes for the eyes.

14

Above the eyes, make 2 larger holes for the horns.

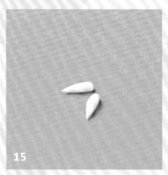

15

For the horns, roll out 2 small white cone shapes.

16

Glue the cones into the holes you made for the horns.

17

Roll 2 small balls of black fondant and glue them into the holes you made for the eyes. Press flat.

18

Open the mouth slightly by pushing the bottom lip down using a needle tool. It doesn't matter if the fondant cracks, since it will be covered.

19

Roll some green fondant and cut out a leaf shape using a small teardrop cutter. Make leaf vein markings with a scalpel.

20

Roll out some green fondant to make grass. Glue the leaf and the grass into the mouth. Don't glue the head in place yet.

TOP TIP

With all characters, mark the position of key features such as eyes, ears, and mouth using a needle tool. Do this early on so that you don't spoil your character at a later stage by gluing something in the wrong place.

21

Cut out 2 large white teardrop shapes and 2 smaller pink ones. Glue a pink teardrop onto a white one and press to flatten.

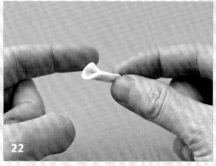

22

Take 1 teardrop shape, and fold as shown; then gently bend back the open end to make an ear.

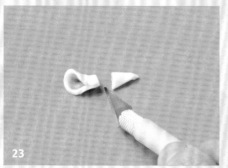

23

Cut off the pointed end using a scalpel. Repeat steps 22–23 to make the other ear.

24

Glue the ears in place just below the horns—they should be wide open. Add any additional black fondant patches to the body.

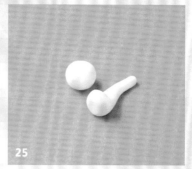

25

To make the legs, roll 2 balls of white fondant and shape into cones.

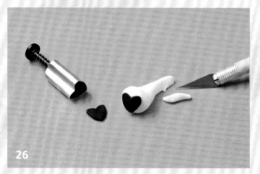

26

Using a small cutter, cut out 2 hearts from black fondant and glue one to the base of each foot. Trim the legs so that they sit close to the body.

27

Glue the legs in place at the base of the body.

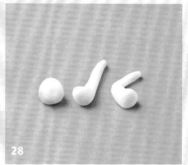

28

For the arms, roll out 2 white balls into cone shapes. Bend each one in the middle to make elbows.

29

Cut out 2 black fondant hearts and glue them to the hands. Attach small patches of black fondant to the arms.

30

Attach the arms to the body using edible glue.

TOP TIP

Always focus on key characteristics. For example, elephants have big ears, cows and giraffes have floppy ears, and cats have pointy ears. It's these features that will define the personality of your creation.

31

When all the parts are in place and you're happy that you have enough black patches, gently lift the head and glue it in position.

32

For the tail, roll out a ball of white fondant into a long, thin sausage and make 5 pointed cones from black fondant.

33

Hold the black pieces and pinch the ends together.

Glue the black piece to one end of the white tail and glue the other end to the back of the cow. Make a tiny flower to attach to her head.

TOP TIP
Always glue your characters to the cake when you have finished, and before you attempt to move it, to prevent them from toppling off when you pick up the cake.

Your finished cow should look like this.

Patches on the cake

Cover your cake in white fondant. Roll out some black fondant, and cut out a random shape with a wavy edge.

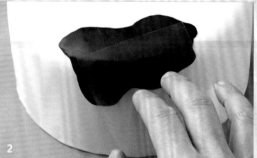

Position the patch on the cake, and smooth down using a cake smoother. You don't need to use glue.

Place patches around the cake, and put a pink (or blue) patch in the center for the cow to sit on. Decorate with flowers and grass as shown.

CAKE DESIGN
I used a cake about 6¼ inches round and 6 inches high (16 cm x 15 cm). The design of the cake was based on the pattern of the cow. I covered the cake in white fondant, then applied the larger black pieces. You could reverse the colors and make the cake black with white patches. Alternatively, use brown and white fondant.

Barnaby
THE SHEEP

You can make this character any size you choose. For the size shown here, use the templates on page 189. The fondant colors for Barnaby are white and black. For the accessories, you will need red, black, white, blue, pink, green, and brown fondant.

YOU WILL NEED:
- Basic modeling kit
  (*see pages 12–13*)
- Fondant (white, black, red, blue, pink, green, and brown)
- Small flower cutters (blossom, jasmine, and daisy)
- Bark imprint mat
- Green royal icing
- Piping bag with grass tip

1

Roll a large white ball for the body and a smaller black ball for the head.

2

Roll the white ball into a cone shape, making sure the narrower end is quite thin.

3

Push a length of spaghetti downward into the fondant to make a support as shown.

4

Roll lots of small white balls, and glue them all over the body, starting at the base. (*See Top Tip on page 157.*)

5

Make sure the spaghetti is still visible when the body is completely covered.

6

Roll the black ball into an egg shape.

7

Position the head on the body—don't add glue at this stage.

8

Use a small ball modeling tool to mark the holes for the eyes.

9

Make nostrils using a needle tool as shown.

10

Use the wide end of a size 2 piping tip to make a smile.

11

To make the eyes, roll 2 small balls of white fondant, and glue them into the holes made in step 8.

12

Add 2 tiny balls of black fondant for the pupils.

13

Roll 5 or 6 small balls of white fondant and glue them to the top of the head.

14

Roll 2 black balls for the ears. Press 1 ball flat between your thumb and finger. Bend it in the middle to make a right angle.

15

Repeat step 14 to make the other ear, then glue both ears in place, either side of the balls on the top of the head.

16

Your sheep should look like this.

17

To make the arms, roll 2 balls of black fondant into cone shapes.

18

Taking 1 of the arms, flatten the wider end to make a hand. Using a scalpel, cut out a small triangle to make a thumb.

19

Use the tip of your finger to soften the edges of the thumb and the hand. Repeat steps 18–19 to make the other arm.

20

Attach the arms to either side of the body using edible glue, then cover the joins with a few more white fondant balls.

21

To make the legs, roll 2 balls of black fondant into long cones.

22

Take 1 leg and pinch the wider end of the cone so that the base is flat. Cut a small groove into the front to create hooves.

23

Bend the leg in the middle to form a right angle; then press the narrow end to flatten. Repeat steps 22–23 to make the other leg.

TOP TIP
To create a more vulnerable and innocent-looking sheep, gently turn the feet inward instead of pointing the toes forward. Nervous characters tend to have their toes pointing inward.

24

Glue the legs underneath the body. You will need to do this on the side of the cake so that the legs can dangle off the side.

Romeo the Reclining Sheep

Romeo's body, head, and legs are made in the same way as for Barnaby, but the legs are attached at a different angle using spaghetti or glue.

25 Your finished sheep should look like this.

For Romeo's arms, follow steps 17–20, opposite, but bend them at the elbows as shown.

3 Romeo should now look like this.

Poppy the Ladybug

For the body, roll out a ball of red fondant into a cone and cut off the narrow end using a scalpel.

Use a wheel tool to make a groove down the middle of the cone.

Roll some small black balls, and glue them to the body; then press flat. Roll a small black ball for the head.

For the eyes, roll 2 small white balls and 2 tiny black balls. Use a size 2 piping tip to make a smile.

For the antennae, glue 2 small black cones onto the head. Bend them carefully.

TOP TIP
Don't be tempted to roll the balls to cover the sheep's body in advance, because they need to be soft in order to fit together and stick in place.

Cedric the Snail

1 Using blue fondant, roll out a sausage shape.

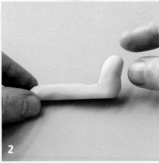

2 Bend the fondant about a third of the way along to make a right angle.

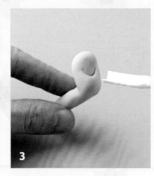

3 Use a smile tool to create a mouth.

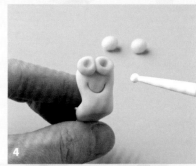

4 For the eyes, roll 2 blue balls and glue them to the face. Using a small ball modeling tool, make an indentation in each eye.

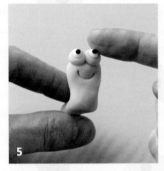

5 Roll 2 small white balls, and push them into the indentations; then add 2 tiny black pupils.

6 To make the shell, roll out a long sausage of darker-blue fondant, then roll it up as shown.

7 Make lines along the shell using a wheel tool.

8 Glue the shell onto the snail's body as shown. Repeat the process in pink to make Winnie, Cedric's girlfriend.

Flowers

1 Make flowers in various colors and shapes using small flower cutters. You need about 100 flowers for an 8-inch (20-cm) cake.

Fence

1 Roll out some brown fondant, and cover with a bark imprint mat. Put pressure on the mat to leave a pattern on the fondant.

2 Cut the fondant into strips of equal length. Make some of the strips pointed at one end to form the vertical sections.

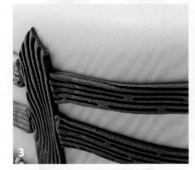

3 Glue the vertical strips in place, spacing them evenly around the cake; then add the horizontal strips.

4 To make the grass, pipe green royal icing or buttercream around the base of the cake using a piping bag with a grass tip.

CAKE DESIGN

For the design opposite, I placed Barnaby and Romeo in a field of flowers. I used a cake about 8 inches round and 4 inches high (20 cm x 10 cm), covering it with green fondant. Fencing and flowers around the cake help to cover the joins. I used grass piping around the base to cover the join between the cake and the board.

Rosie
THE PIG

You can make this character any size you choose. For the size shown, use the templates on page 189. The fondant colors for the pig are pink, white and black. For the accessories, you will need fondant in green, blue and a variety of colors for flowers such as purple, yellow, orange, and red. You will also need green gum paste.

YOU WILL NEED:
- Basic modeling kit (*see pages 12–13*)
- Fondant (pink, white, black, green, and blue)
- Green gum paste
- Selection of flower cutters
- Green royal icing
- Piping bag with grass tip

1. Roll 2 balls of pink fondant for the body and the head.

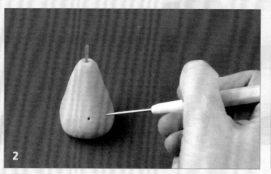

2. Roll the large ball into a cone, and press down in the middle, on one side, to make a tummy. Insert a piece of spaghetti. Make a belly button using a needle tool.

TOP TIP
To make a fondant pig, use a fairly pale pink. There is no other color to break up a brighter shade and a light pink gives a prettier finish.

3. Roll the smaller ball into a rounded cone shape as shown.

TOP TIP
Try to avoid gluing 2 ball shapes together. Flattening the side of each ball that you want to attach will create a wider surface area for gluing. This will make your character more sturdy and less likely to come apart when being moved around.

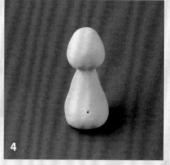

4. Position the head on the body to check the proportions (don't add glue at this stage).

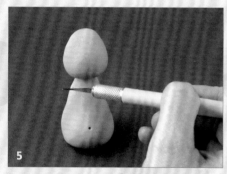

5. Using the back of a scalpel, make small creases for the folds in the skin underneath the arms (which will be added later).

6. For the legs, roll 2 balls of pink fondant into long droplet shapes.

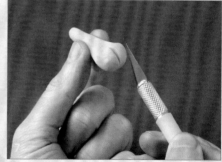

7. Take 1 leg and use a scalpel to make a groove in the wider end to mark the foot. Repeat with the second leg.

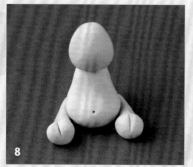

8. Glue the legs in position.

9. To make the arms, roll 2 balls (smaller than those you used for the legs) and shape them into long droplets, but turn up the wider end a little.

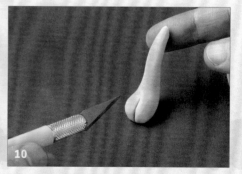

10. Take 1 arm and make a groove, using your scalpel, to mark the foot. Repeat with the other arm.

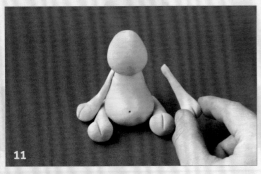

11

Glue the arms in place, ensuring that the feet are pointing forward on the work surface.

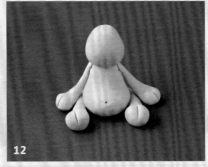

12

Your pig should now look like this.

13

Roll out some pink fondant to a thickness of about ¼ inch (5 mm). Cut out an oval shape for the snout.

14

Glue the snout onto the face, covering the nose and mouth area.

15

To make the ears, roll 2 small fondant balls. Pinch one end with your thumb and finger to make a point.

16

Take 1 ear, and cut off the rounded end, leaving a soft-edged triangle. Make a groove in the ear to show a fold.

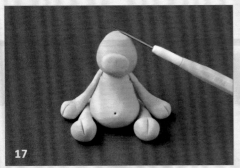

17

Make a slot with a needle tool for the ear to fit into.

18

Repeat steps 16–17 to make the other ear; then glue both ears in place.

19

Use a small ball modeling tool to make 2 indents for the nostrils. Ensure that these are central.

20

Roll 2 small white fondant balls for the eyes, and use a needle tool to mark their position on the face.

21

Glue the eyes in place, and add 2 tiny black fondant balls for the pupils.

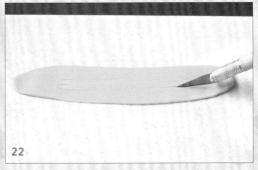

22

Roll out a piece of green gum paste, and cut 2 strips about ¼ inch (5 mm) wide.

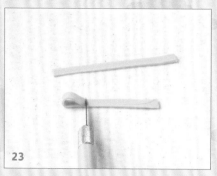

23 Lightly fold over the end of 1 strip. Decide how big you want the loop to be; then mark the position on the fondant.

24 Unfold the strip, and use the mark you have made to work out how long the other end of the bow should be. Cut off the excess.

25 Apply glue over the mark.

26 Fold in the 2 ends of the strip so that they sit on the mark.

27 Use the other strip to cover the join by wrapping it around the center of the bow. Glue in place; then trim off the ends.

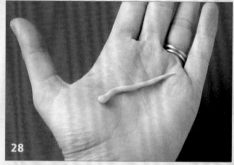

28 To make a curly tail, roll out a thin sausage of pink fondant.

29 Wind the tail around a paintbrush handle and leave it to set for 10 minutes.

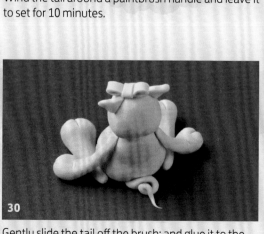

30 Gently slide the tail off the brush; and glue it to the back of the pig.

31 Your finished pig should look like this.

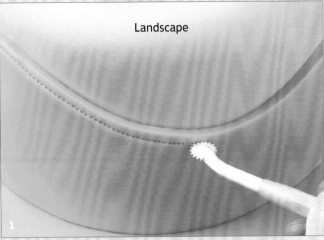

Landscape

Cover your cake board with green fondant and your cake with blue fondant. Place a wavy, green strip around the sides of the cake to make hills. Roll a stitching tool around the edges of the hills.

TOP TIP

A rotary stitching tool is an excellent implement for cake designing. You can use it alongside a needle tool to create a stitching pattern, giving your cake a simple retro look. This adds another level of interest to the design.

Use a selection of flower cutters to make a variety of flowers, and glue them onto the green fondant. Cut long green triangles to make the stems and glue them in place.

Use a needle tool to make a line of dots around the flowers, replicating the effect of the stitching tool. For large straight areas, use the stitching tool.

To cover the join between the cake and the board, pipe green royal icing or buttercream around the base of the cake with a grass tip. Decorate with flowers and grass as desired.

CAKE DESIGN

For the design shown opposite, you need a very tall cake so that you have a base on which to create a landscape. The cake was approximately 8 inches round and 9½ inches high (20 cm x 24 cm) in depth. If you put the cake on a large board, you can place little characters all around the cake landscape. I have clouds and a sun in the sky, but you could add a little house, car, or tree on the horizon.

Oscar
THE CAT

You can make this character any size you choose. For the size shown, use the templates on page 188. The fondant colors for Oscar are gray, red, pink, white, black, and blue. For the accessories, you will need white, black, pink, brown, and eucalyptus fondant and white gum paste.

YOU WILL NEED:
- Basic modeling kit (*see pages 12–13*)
- Fondant (gray, red, pink, white, black, brown, eucalyptus, and blue)
- 28-gauge floral wire
- Edible dusting powder in pink, white, brown, and purple
- Small rectangular cutter
- Pink, white, and green gel paste food coloring
- Wax paper
- White gum paste
- Metallic silver edible paint

1

Roll 2 balls of light-gray fondant for the body and the head.

2

Roll the larger ball into a cone shape, making sure that it's quite thin at the smaller end.

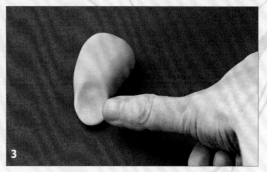

3

Lay the cone on your work surface and flatten the smaller end with your thumb.

4

Roll the smaller ball into an egg shape.

5

Mark the position of the ears with a needle tool.

6

Gently draw the top of the mouth with a scalpel. Mark the eyes using a needle tool.

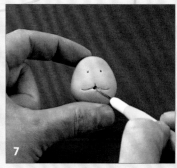

7

Use the needle tool to make a large hole in the center of the mouth where the tongue will be inserted.

8

For the tongue, make a red cone, flatten it, and then cut off the point. Score a line down the middle.

9

Glue the tongue in place as shown.

10

For the nose, make a pink cone shape. Cut off and discard the rounded end.

11

Glue the nose in position as shown.

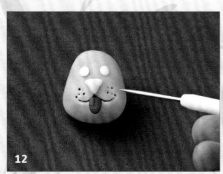

12

Make holes for whiskers using a needle tool.

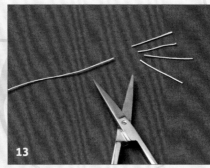

13

Cut 6 x ¾-inch-long (2 cm) pieces of 28-gauge floral wire. (*See Top Tip, page 168.*)

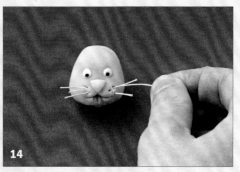

14

Push the wire or noodles into the holes.

15 For the ears, roll 2 gray balls. Using your finger and thumb, pinch one end of each ball to make a cone.

16 Take 1 cone and flatten, then cut off and discard the rounded end. Cut out a pink triangle.

17 Glue the triangle into the ear; then repeat steps 16–17 to make the other ear.

18 Glue the ears into the slots made in step 5.

TOP TIP
As an edible alternative for whiskers, you could use rice noodles instead of floral wire.

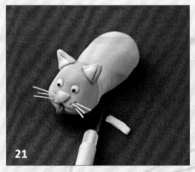

19 Glue the head onto the flattened end of the body.

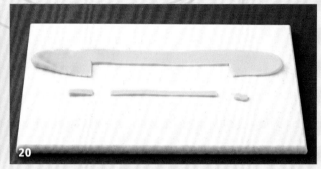

20 Cut a strip of light-blue fondant to make a collar.

21 Apply glue behind the neck and secure the collar over the join. Remove any excess fondant.

22 To make the back legs, roll 2 balls of gray fondant into cones, making them slightly curved.

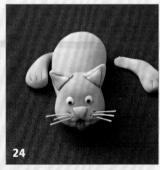

23 Take 1 leg, and make 3 grooves in the wide end of the cone to form a paw.

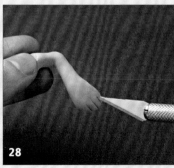

24 Repeat step 23 for the other leg, ensuring the paw faces the other way. Glue the legs in place.

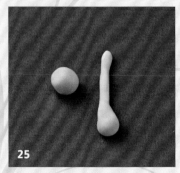

25 To make the arms, roll out 2 balls of fondant into long cone shapes as shown.

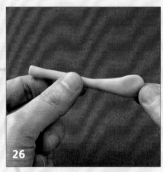

26 Take 1 arm and flatten the wider end of the cone, turning it slightly as you do so.

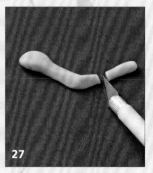

27 Bend the arm to create an elbow. Cut the fondant ½ inch (1 cm) above the elbow.

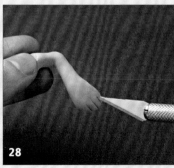

28 Make 3 grooves in the paw. Repeat steps 26–28 for the other arm, making sure it faces the other way.

29

30

31

Glue the arms in place. While the fondant is still soft, make a ball shape in which to slot the mouse under one paw.

Slot the mouse into the cat's paw (see below for how to make the mouse).

For the tail, roll a long cone and bend the wider end as shown. Create a wave in the tail, and flatten the wide end.

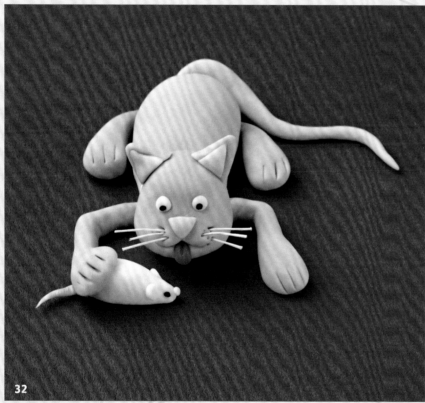

32

Glue the tail in place underneath the cat's rump. Your finished cat should look like this.

Milo the Mouse

1

Roll out a ball of white fondant into a cone and gently pinch the pointed end.

2

For the ears, roll 2 tiny white balls, and place them in the correct position as shown. Gently press and smooth them into place with a small ball modeling tool.

3

Add 2 tiny black fondant balls for eyes and a pink ball for the nose. Dust the ears and the sides of the body with light-pink edible dusting powder.

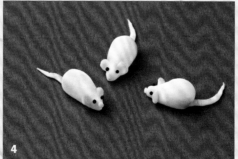

4

To make a tail, roll out a thin cone of light-pink fondant and mark lines along it with the back of a scalpel. Make as many mice as you wish.

TOP TIP
As an alternative to using tiny balls of fondant to make eyes, why not use nonpareils (sugar sprinkles) in an appropriate color?

Floorboards

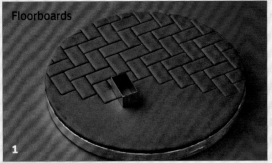

1

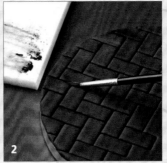

2

TOP TIP
Dark-purple edible dusting powder is perfect for dark shadows. You can use it for everything from lines in floors to shadows under eyes. Always use dark purple rather than black—black tends to be too harsh.

Cover a cake board in brown fondant; then gently use a rectangle cutter to make a herringbone pattern all over the surface of the fondant.

Dust over the lines with brown edible dusting powder; then darken the lines themselves with purple dusting powder.

Wallpaper

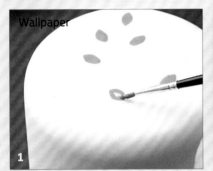

1

2

3

Using gel paste food coloring and a size 2 artist's paintbrush, paint light-pink petals on the surface of your cake.

Using a size 1 or 2 artist's paintbrush, paint darker lines around the base of each petal to make a "V" shape.

Join the petals by using green gel paste food coloring mixed with water. If the green is too dark, add a little yellow gel paste food coloring.

Baseboard and mouse door

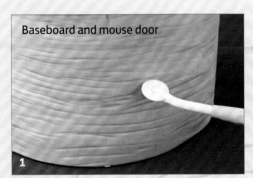

1

2

3

Wrap eucalyptus-colored fondant around the cake base. Make lines using a wheel tool and dust on light pink, brown, and yellow edible dusting powder.

Make a door template out of wax paper. Cut out a door using brown fondant. Make vertical lines using a wheel tool.

Glue the door in place and make some softer lines with the wheel tool to give the appearance of wood.

4

5

CAKE DESIGN
For the design opposite, I made a cake 6¼ inches round and 8 inches high (16 cm x 20 cm). The cake sits on a large round 13-inch (33-cm) board so that there is enough space for the mice to sit next to the cake. The floor is intentionally haphazard to create a rustic effect.

Glue 2 more strips of brown fondant around the door frame and add lines with the wheel tool.

Using gum paste, make a white doorknob and 2 hinges, then paint them with light-silver or gold metallic paint.

Monty
THE HORSE

Make this character any size you choose. For the size shown here, use the templates on page 188. Fondant colors for Monty are brown, beige, white, black, and blue. The accessory colors are red, green, brown, gray, black, white, and yellow fondant, and white and brown gum paste.

Roll 2 balls of brown fondant for the body and the head.

Roll the larger ball into a cone, making sure the bottom end is much bigger than the top.

Using your thumb, press down the front, in the middle, to make a fat belly.

Insert a piece of spaghetti as shown, then make a belly button using a needle tool.

Roll the smaller ball into an egg shape.

TOP TIP
Cows and horses are made in very similar ways. The main difference is that the horse's head is longer and thinner than the cow's. A horse's head is similar in length to a dog's.

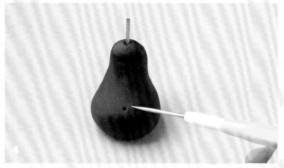

Position the head on the spaghetti to check that it's in proportion with the body.

Roll out some beige fondant, and cut out an oval shape about the same size as the front of the face.

Glue the oval to the face as shown; then smooth out the edges.

Using a small ball modeling tool, make 2 indentations for the nostrils.

Use the wide end of a size 2 piping tip to make a smile.

Mark 2 holes for the eyes using a needle tool; then use the side of the needle tool to make grooves where the ears will sit.

Roll 2 balls of white fondant, and glue them over the holes you made for the eyes.

Roll 2 small black fondant balls for the pupils, and glue them in place.

To make the ears, roll 2 balls of brown fondant. Take 1 ball, and pinch it between your thumb and finger to make a triangle.

Squash the fondant flat, and cut off the rounded end. Make a smaller beige triangle, and glue this onto the center of the brown triangle.

Repeat steps 14–15 to make the other ear (make sure they're the same size).

Glue the ears in place in the grooves you made in step 11.

TOP TIP
The eyes dictate the personality of your characters. To make them look cute, point the eyes up to one side. For a mischievous or patronizing look, angle them down to one side. For intelligence, point the eyes forward. For craziness, make them cross-eyed!

Cut 4 strips of blue fondant (this includes some spares, in case you break any).

Glue 1 strip of fondant over the seam around the nose.

Glue another strip around the back of the head; then join it to the first strip at the sides.

To cover the join, roll a small ball of blue fondant, and glue it in place.

Using a scalpel, mark a cross on the blue ball.

To make the hair, roll out some small, pointed cones of beige fondant; then glue them in place between the ears.

TOP TIP
When working with brown fondant, I usually add a small amount of white. This is because pure brown tends to be very dark and makes it difficult to see the detail on the features.

To make the legs, roll out 2 balls of brown fondant into cones.

Glue a circle of beige fondant onto the wide end of each cone.

To make the horseshoes, use a teardrop cutter to cut 2 blue fondant shapes.

Using a smaller teardrop cutter, cut a piece out of the center of the 2 larger shapes.

Use a scalpel to cut off the pointed ends, to make 2 horseshoes.

Glue the horseshoes to the beige circles, and mark little holes around the shoes with a needle tool.

Glue the legs in place on either side of the body. You could also glue the head in position at this point.

TOP TIP
Always plan the full design of your cake before you start. This way you will ensure that all characters are looking in the correct direction and are in proportion with each other. As a rule of thumb, the average height of a character on a cake is 3¼ inches (8 cm); on a cupcake it's 2 inches (5 cm).

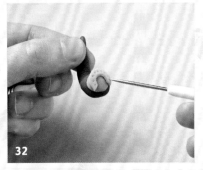

To make the arms, roll out 2 balls of brown fondant into a cone. Bend each one in the middle to make a right angle.

Repeat steps 26–29 to make 2 more horseshoes.

Glue the arms in place so they are resting on the legs.

To make the hair, use a sugarcraft extruder gun with a multistrand hair disc.

Roll out a sausage of beige fondant, and insert it into the craft extruder gun. Screw on the disc.

TOP TIP
When using a craft extruder gun with fondant, add extra white vegetable shortening to the fondant before you put it in the gun. This prevents the gun from drying out the fondant as it squeezes it out.

Pump out the hair until it's the length you require. Use your fingers to break it from the gun, and attach the strands at one end to make a tail.

Glue the tail to the back of the horse so that he's sitting on it. Your horse is now finished.

Apples

Roll balls of red and green fondant, and make a small indentation in the top of each one using a ball modeling tool. Roll out some short cones of brown fondant, and glue one in each indentation.

Bucket

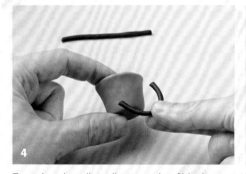

TOP TIP
Do as much modeling as you can using just your fingers; only use a tool when necessary to make the shape more accurate.

Roll a ball of gray fondant into a cone. Cut off the top and bottom of the cone.

Using your thumb and finger, pinch around the edge of the wide surface to make a rim.

To make a handle, roll out a strip of black gum paste, and bend it into a curve. Allow it to dry for 10 minutes.

While the gum paste is drying, finish the bucket. Tap the top against your work surface to make it level.

Using a large ball modeling tool, push the fondant against your finger to make a rim.

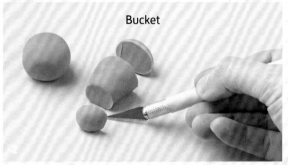

Attach the handle to the bucket; then add some of your apples (you may need to glue these in place).

Fence

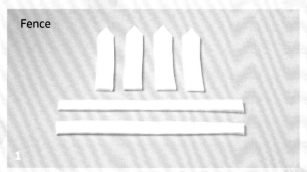

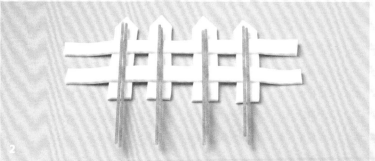

To make the fence, roll out 2 long strips of white gum paste and 4 shorter strips with a point cut at the tip. Glue the long strips on top of the shorter strips.

To hold the strips together, glue 2 or 3 pieces of spaghetti to the back of the shorter strips of fondant.

Turn over the fence. To avoid breaking it when you push it into the cake, make little holes in the top of your cake in line with the spaghetti. Glue the fence to the top of your cake.

CAKE DESIGN
In the picture opposite, I have set the horse beside a small barn on a large 12-inch (30-cm) round cake. The barn is made from 2 rectangular cakes, with the roof carved from cake. The cakes are covered in red and brown fondant.

Barn

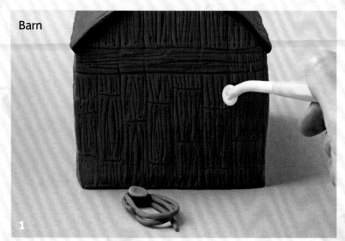

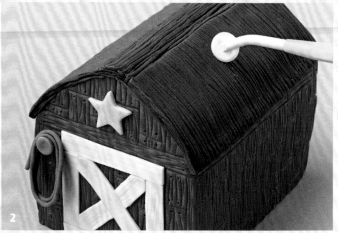

Cover your cake in red fondant and use a wheel tool to make wood markings (lots of small irregular lines will look very effective). Make a roof using brown fondant.

Add marks to the roof, as in step 1. Attach a door made from white strips, a star, and a length of gum paste rolled up to look like rope. Glue the rope to a small knob of gray fondant and attach to the barn.

Templates

If you want to make your characters the same size as those shown in the book, use these templates as a guide.

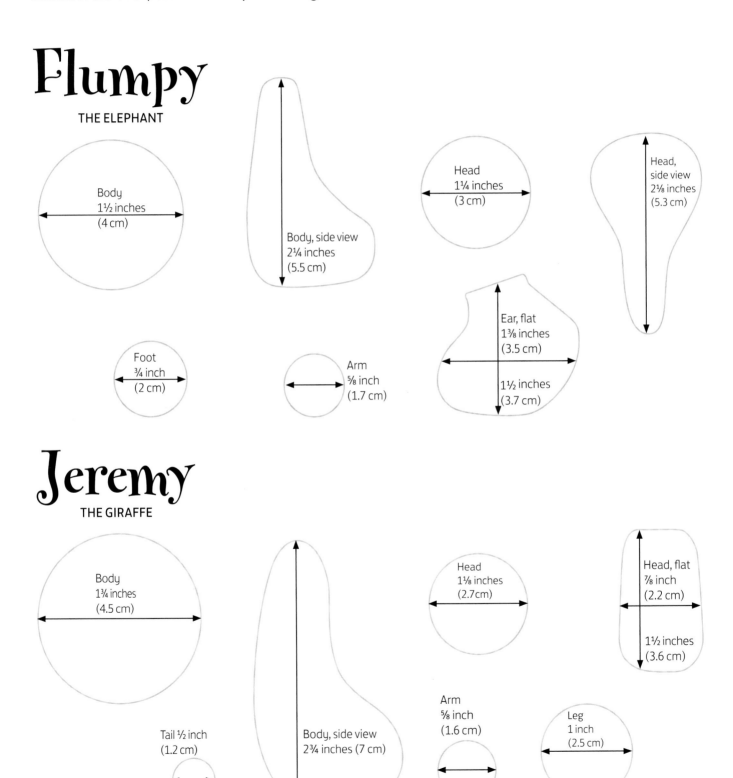

Flumpy
THE ELEPHANT

Body
1½ inches
(4 cm)

Body, side view
2¼ inches
(5.5 cm)

Head
1¼ inches
(3 cm)

Head,
side view
2⅛ inches
(5.3 cm)

Foot
¾ inch
(2 cm)

Arm
⅝ inch
(1.7 cm)

Ear, flat
1⅜ inches
(3.5 cm)

1½ inches
(3.7 cm)

Jeremy
THE GIRAFFE

Body
1¾ inches
(4.5 cm)

Head
1⅛ inches
(2.7cm)

Head, flat
⅞ inch
(2.2 cm)

1½ inches
(3.6 cm)

Tail ½ inch
(1.2 cm)

Body, side view
2¾ inches (7 cm)

Arm
⅝ inch
(1.6 cm)

Leg
1 inch
(2.5 cm)

Maloo

THE MONKEY

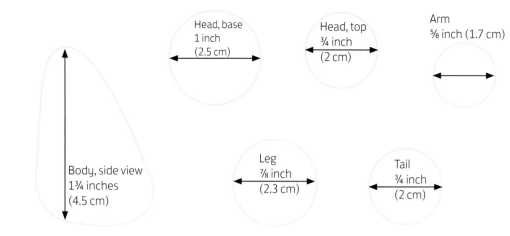

Body
1½ inches
(4 cm)

Body, side view
1¾ inches
(4.5 cm)

Head, base
1 inch
(2.5 cm)

Head, top
¾ inch
(2 cm)

Arm
⅝ inch (1.7 cm)

Leg
⅞ inch
(2.3 cm)

Tail
¾ inch
(2 cm)

Ariel

THE LION

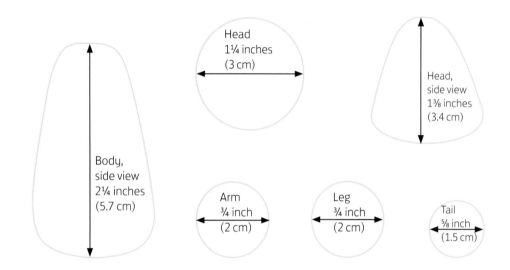

Body
1¾ inches
(4.3 cm)

Body,
side view
2¼ inches
(5.7 cm)

Head
1¼ inches
(3 cm)

Head,
side view
1⅜ inches
(3.4 cm)

Arm
¾ inch
(2 cm)

Leg
¾ inch
(2 cm)

Tail
⅝ inch
(1.5 cm)

Zachary

THE ZEBRA

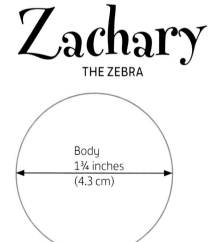

Body
1¾ inches
(4.3 cm)

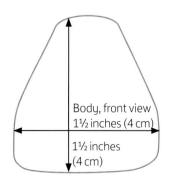

Body, front view
1½ inches (4 cm)

1½ inches
(4 cm)

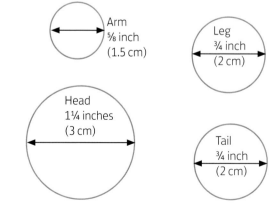

Arm
⅝ inch
(1.5 cm)

Leg
¾ inch
(2 cm)

Head
1¼ inches
(3 cm)

Tail
¾ inch
(2 cm)

Eden

THE FAIRY

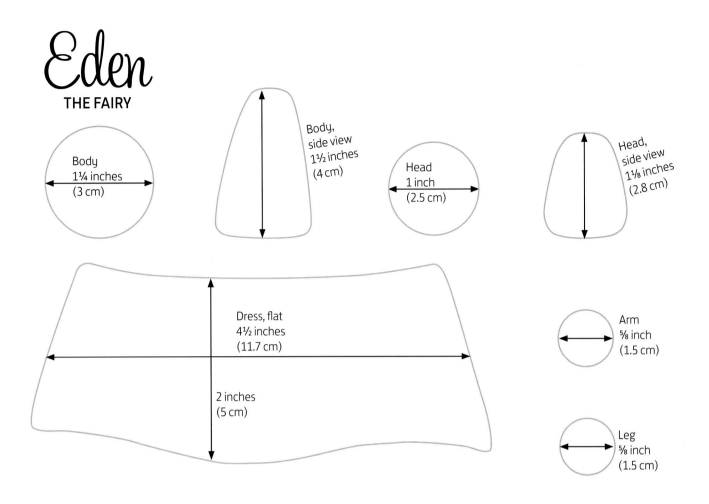

Body
1¼ inches
(3 cm)

Body,
side view
1½ inches
(4 cm)

Head
1 inch
(2.5 cm)

Head,
side view
1⅛ inches
(2.8 cm)

Dress, flat
4½ inches
(11.7 cm)

2 inches
(5 cm)

Arm
⅝ inch
(1.5 cm)

Leg
⅝ inch
(1.5 cm)

Darcie

THE FAIRY

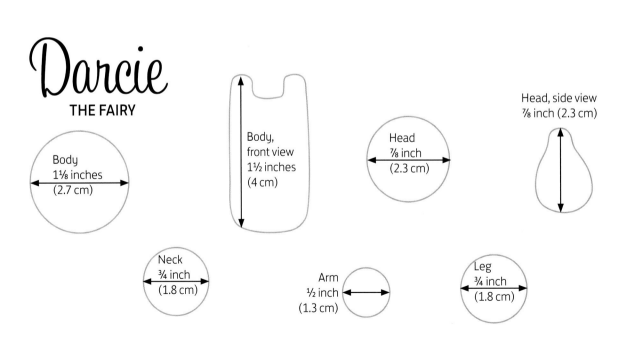

Body
1⅛ inches
(2.7 cm)

Body,
front view
1½ inches
(4 cm)

Head
⅞ inch
(2.3 cm)

Head, side view
⅞ inch (2.3 cm)

Neck
¾ inch
(1.8 cm)

Arm
½ inch
(1.3 cm)

Leg
¾ inch
(1.8 cm)

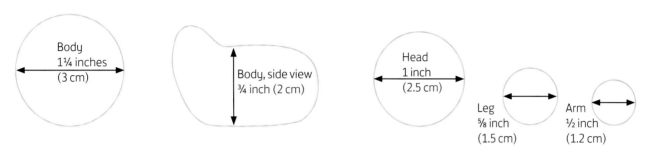

Matilda

THE FAIRY

Body
1¼ inches
(3 cm)

Body, side view
¾ inch (2 cm)

Head
1 inch
(2.5 cm)

Leg
⅝ inch
(1.5 cm)

Arm
½ inch
(1.2 cm)

Bramble & Ben

THE FAIRIES

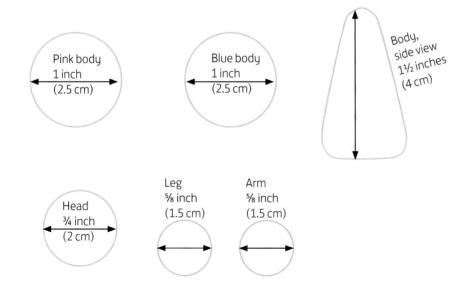

Pink body
1 inch
(2.5 cm)

Blue body
1 inch
(2.5 cm)

Body,
side view
1½ inches
(4 cm)

Head
¾ inch
(2 cm)

Leg
⅝ inch
(1.5 cm)

Arm
⅝ inch
(1.5 cm)

Gooba
THE ALIEN

Body
1⅜ inches
(3.5 cm)

Body,
side view
1½ inches
(4 cm)

Arm
⅝ inch
(1.5 cm)

Head
1¼ inches
(3 cm)

Leg
¾ inch
(2 cm)

Head,
side view
1¼ inches
(3 cm)

Blinky
THE ALIEN

Foot
½ inch
(1.2 cm)

Eye
⅝ inch
(1.5 cm)

Arm
⅝ inch
(1.5 cm)

Body
¼ inch (0.5 cm)

Head
1¼ inches
(3 cm)

Boppa
THE MONSTER

Body
1¾ inches
(4.5 cm)

Arm
⅝ inch
(1.5 cm)

Eye
⅞ inch
(2.2 cm)

Leg
⅞ inch
(2.2 cm)

Bertie
THE ALIEN

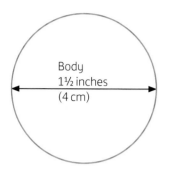

Body
1½ inches
(4 cm)

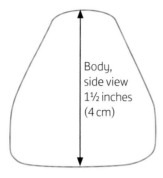

Body,
side view
1½ inches
(4 cm)

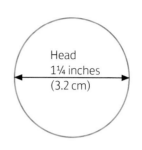

Head
1¼ inches
(3.2 cm)

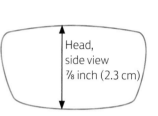

Head,
side view
⅞ inch (2.3 cm)

Eye
¾ inch
(2 cm)

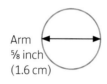

Arm
⅝ inch
(1.6 cm)

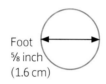

Foot
⅝ inch
(1.6 cm)

Tail
½ inch
(1.3 cm)

Giggles
THE MONSTER

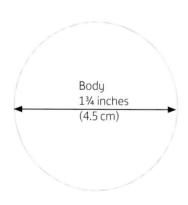

Body
1¾ inches
(4.5 cm)

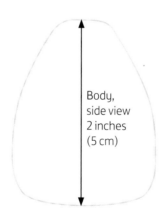

Body,
side view
2 inches
(5 cm)

Leg
⅝ inch
(1.5 cm)

Arm
⅝ inch
(1.5 cm)

ROXY

THE OCTOPUS

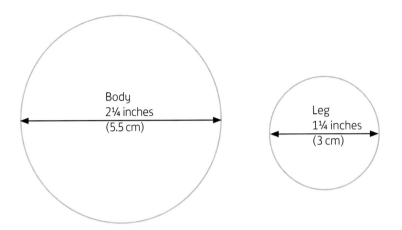

Body
2¼ inches
(5.5 cm)

Leg
1¼ inches
(3 cm)

Leg length 6¼ inches
(16 cm)

TONTO

THE TURTLE

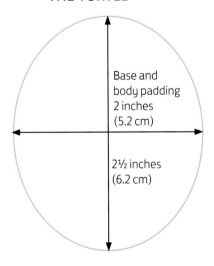

Base and
body padding
2 inches
(5.2 cm)

2½ inches
(6.2 cm)

Neck
¾ inch
(2 cm)

Head
1⅜ inches
(3.5 cm)

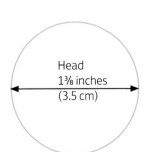

Head,
side view
1¾ inches
(4.3 cm)

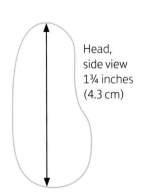

Arm
¾ inch
(1.8 cm)

Leg
⅝ inch
(1.5 cm)

CHARLIE

THE PARROT

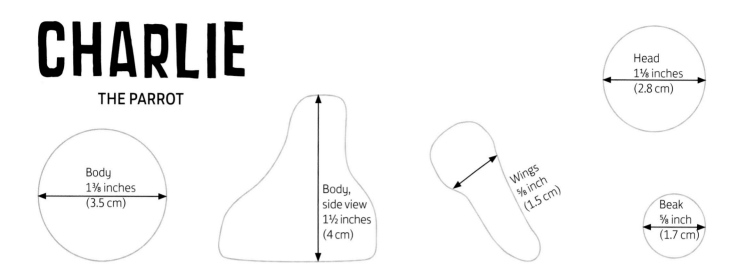

Body
1⅜ inches
(3.5 cm)

Body,
side view
1½ inches
(4 cm)

Wings
⅝ inch
(1.5 cm)

Head
1⅛ inches
(2.8 cm)

Beak
⅝ inch
(1.7 cm)

BOOMER

THE FISH

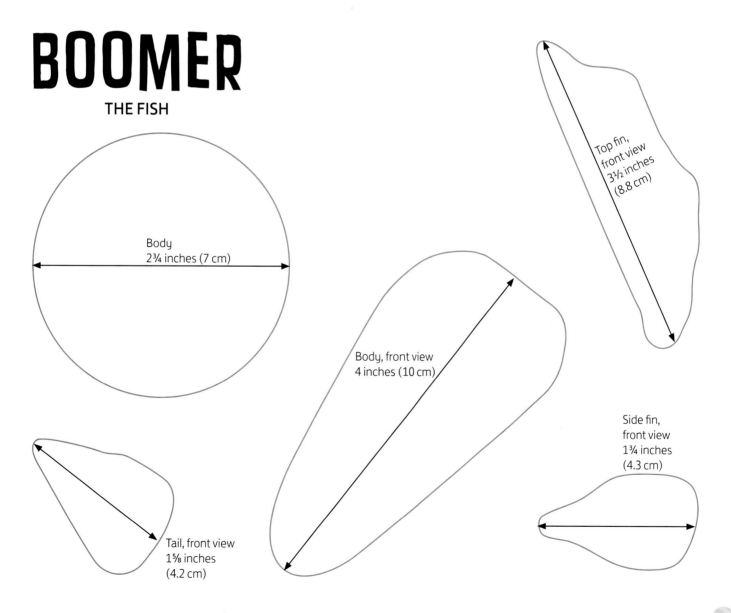

Body
2¾ inches (7 cm)

Top fin,
front view
3½ inches
(8.8 cm)

Body, front view
4 inches (10 cm)

Side fin,
front view
1¾ inches
(4.3 cm)

Tail, front view
1⅝ inches
(4.2 cm)

Monty
THE HORSE

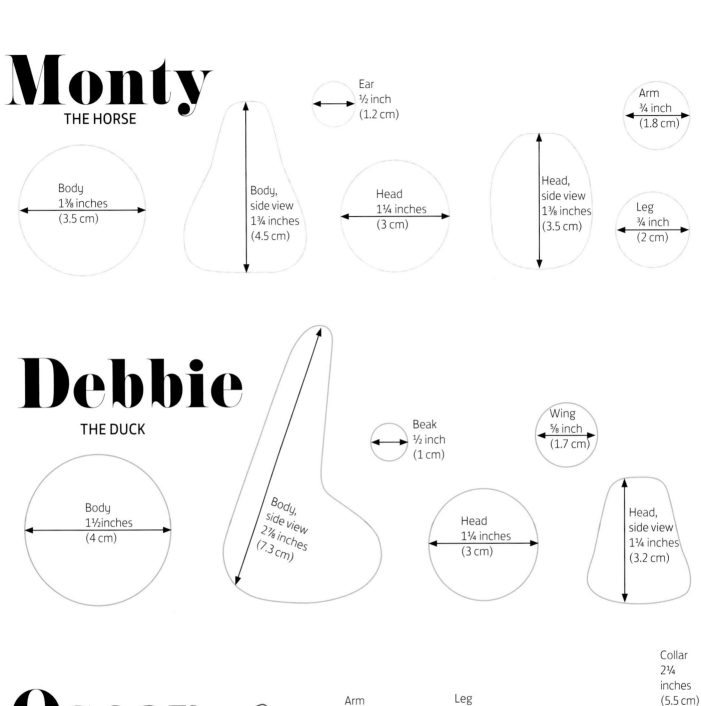

Ear
½ inch
(1.2 cm)

Arm
¾ inch
(1.8 cm)

Body
1⅜ inches
(3.5 cm)

Body,
side view
1¾ inches
(4.5 cm)

Head
1¼ inches
(3 cm)

Head,
side view
1⅜ inches
(3.5 cm)

Leg
¾ inch
(2 cm)

Debbie
THE DUCK

Beak
½ inch
(1 cm)

Wing
⅝ inch
(1.7 cm)

Body
1½ inches
(4 cm)

Body,
side view
2⅞ inches
(7.3 cm)

Head
1¼ inches
(3 cm)

Head,
side view
1¼ inches
(3.2 cm)

Oscar
THE CAT

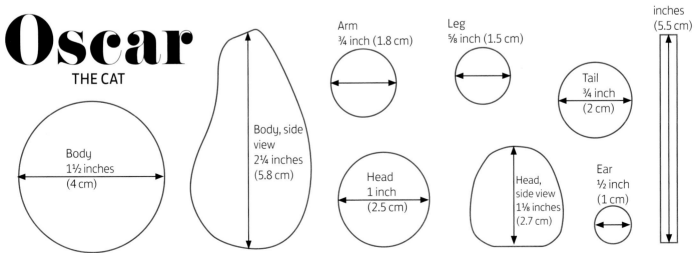

Arm
¾ inch (1.8 cm)

Leg
⅝ inch (1.5 cm)

Collar
2¼
inches
(5.5 cm)

Body
1½ inches
(4 cm)

Body, side
view
2¼ inches
(5.8 cm)

Tail
¾ inch
(2 cm)

Head
1 inch
(2.5 cm)

Head,
side view
1⅛ inches
(2.7 cm)

Ear
½ inch
(1 cm)

Barnaby
THE SHEEP

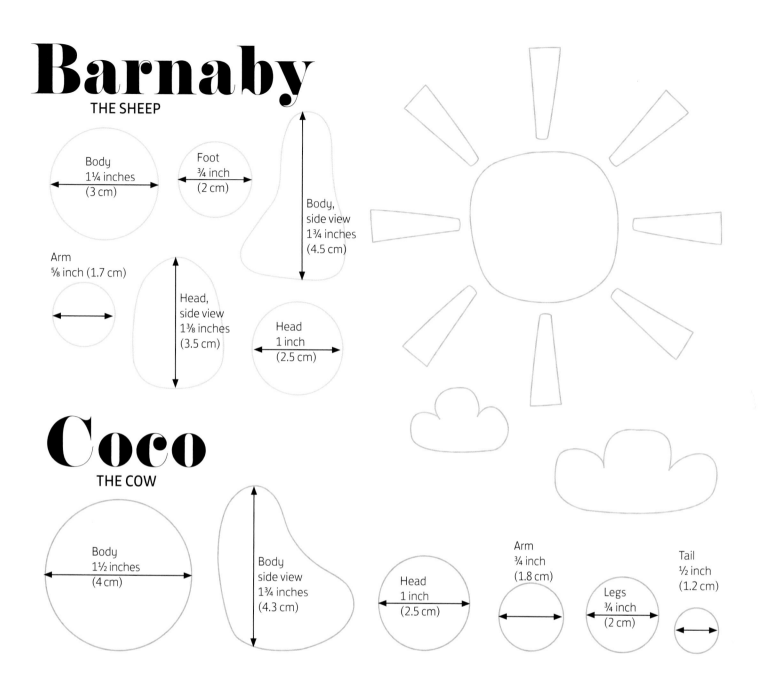

Body
1¼ inches
(3 cm)

Foot
¾ inch
(2 cm)

Body,
side view
1¾ inches
(4.5 cm)

Arm
⅝ inch (1.7 cm)

Head,
side view
1⅜ inches
(3.5 cm)

Head
1 inch
(2.5 cm)

Coco
THE COW

Body
1½ inches
(4 cm)

Body
side view
1¾ inches
(4.3 cm)

Head
1 inch
(2.5 cm)

Arm
¾ inch
(1.8 cm)

Legs
¾ inch
(2 cm)

Tail
½ inch
(1.2 cm)

Rosie
THE PIG

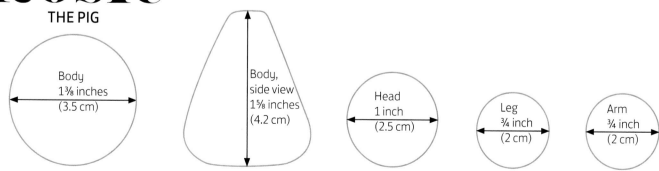

Body
1⅜ inches
(3.5 cm)

Body,
side view
1⅝ inches
(4.2 cm)

Head
1 inch
(2.5 cm)

Leg
¾ inch
(2 cm)

Arm
¾ inch
(2 cm)

SUPPLIERS

Everything used in this book is available from specialist cake-decorating suppliers and, increasingly, in supermarkets. You can also purchase everything you need for cake decorating and modeling in the Pretty Witty Cakes online shop, which ships products all over the world. You can find us at **www.prettywittycakes.co.uk**.

We also teach online cake-decorating classes that are available 24 hours a day, 7 days a week, anywhere in the world. Suzi and her team of around 20 tutors present everything from basic baking to advanced cake-making and decorating. There are members of the online tutorial site located all around the world in over 47 countries. To become a member of the online tutorial site, visit **www.prettywittycakes.co.uk**.

Throughout the year, we also host live classes and private one-to-one classes, and Suzi is a regular demonstrator and guest speaker at international cake shows.

INDEX

To my husband and best friend, James, who has given me all the support I could ever wish for.

This book has been such fun to create, and many memories will remain with me forever.

I would like to thank everyone who works at Pretty Witty Cakes, who have enabled me to spend time working on this book. In particular, I want to give special thanks to Amber, who makes my life so much easier every day in the kitchen, and for her contribution to sections of this book. I also want to thank Kate, whose hard work and loyalty have enabled me to devote hundreds of hours to this book, knowing that my inbox was in safe hands.

I would also like to thank my publisher and the team at Quadrille: Alison Cathie, Jane O' Shea, and Lisa Pendreigh. A very special thanks to Nikki Ellis, who was with me from beginning to end of writing this book and whose enthusiasm was truly infectious. I also appreciated the fact that Nikki never failed to come to all our meetings armed with packs of cookies, and patiently assisted and provided invaluable advice on all those tiny details in the images.

A very big thank-you goes to my fabulous photography team, who were often working long into the night on our photo shoots. I shall have memories of chewy fish candy and the amazing Malou Burger forever. To be able to work with a team who makes you laugh so much, especially on such long days, was an absolute privilege. Special thanks also go to Sheila Udeagu, who was a total joy to work with, as well as Polly Webb-Wilson and Tom and Ben.

I would also like to thank Katie Golsby for her guidance and expertise in editing the copy in the book and for patiently waiting for me to reply to her emails. Her advice on text layout was so helpful.

With so many teachers now teaching at Pretty Witty Cakes, I have been privileged to be able to talk about my ideas with some amazing cake-makers and learn from many others. I would like to make special thanks to my good friend Kaysie Lackey, who first introduced me to color shapers in 2011. I would also like to thank the lovely Rachel Hill, who is not only a great cake-maker but also a friend and someone who has given me guidance and advice. Thank you, May Clee Cadman, for your pearls of wisdom about writing cake books.

I would also like to take a special opportunity to thank Hannah, who helps me juggle motherhood with business, letting me know at times when I was working that my children were well cared for and happy.

Most of all, a heartfelt thank-you to all our customers who have supported us, both past and present. I met so many of you in 2010 when I started the business, and so many of you remain loyal customers to this day—and, for that, I thank you from the bottom of my heart.

I would also like to thank several of my amazing suppliers, who have delivered things to me at short notice and often offered me sound business advice. Particular mention goes to Mike and Karen of FPC Sugarcraft.

A very special thank-you goes to some of my lifelong friends, who watched me start Pretty Witty Cakes from scratch and have given me the strength and support that only friends can give. Special thanks in particular go to Dave Hall: one of the most talented artists I have ever met and the only person who can take my words and turn them into an exact picture of what is in my head. Special thanks also go to Phillip Hall, who, from the other side of the world, has offered sound business and personal advice to me from the day I started Pretty Witty Cakes.

Finally, I would like to thank my husband, James, and my two children, Barnaby and Bertie. I am so privileged to have them as my family, and although my family is small, it is the best little family in the world. I could not wish for a better and more supportive husband or two more beautiful and loving children. Every character and cake I make starts and ends with you.

First edition for the United States and Canada published in 2015 by Barron's Educational Series, Inc.

First published in 2014 by Quadrille Publishing Ltd
Pentagon House, 52–54 Southwark Street, London SE1 1UN
www.quadrille.co.uk

Text and character design © 2014 Suzi Witt
Photography © 2014 Malou Burger
Design and layout © 2014 Quadrille Publishing Ltd

PUBLISHING DIRECTOR Jane O'Shea
COMMISSIONING EDITOR Lisa Pendreigh
PROJECT EDITOR Katie Golsby
CREATIVE DIRECTOR Helen Lewis
SENIOR DESIGNER Nicola Ellis
DESIGN ASSISTANT Emily Lapworth
PHOTOGRAPHER Malou Burger
STYLIST Polly Webb-Wilson
PRODUCTION DIRECTOR Vincent Smith
PRODUCTION CONTROLLER Sarah Neesam

All inquiries should be addressed to:
Barron's Educational Series, Inc.
250 Wireless Boulevard
Hauppauge, New York 11788
www.barronseduc.com

ISBN: 978-1-4380-0736-6

Library of Congress Control No.: 2014957222

Printed in China

9 8 7 6 5 4 3 2 1